HURT PEOPLE HURT PEOPLE

GOD'S HOPE AND HEALING FOR YOU AND YOUR RELATIONSHIPS

DR. SANDRA D. WILSON

Our Daily Bread
Publishing.

Hurt People Hurt People: God's Hope and Healing for You and Your Relationships
© 2001 by Sandra D. Wilson
Updated edition © 2025 by Sandra D. Wilson

ISBN: 978-1-64070-398-8

Library of Congress Cataloging-in-Publication Data Available

Printed in the United States of America
25 26 27 28 29 30 31 32 / 8 7 6 5 4 3 2 1

With inexpressible love and gratitude,
I dedicate this book to my Savior and Lord,
Jesus Christ, the Healer of all hurts.

CONTENTS

Contents

INTRODUCTION

It's true, isn't it? Hurt people hurt people.

All of us have been hurt by people who all were hurt by other hurt people. In turn, we—as hurt people—all have hurt other people to one degree or another. And on and on it goes.

Admittedly, I am stretching the word *hurt* very broadly. By *hurts* I mean actions, words, and attitudes that are intentional or unintentional, visible or invisible, hands-on or hands-off, perpetrated by others or self-inflicted, that range from barely survivable to hardly noticeable.

The resulting wounds and injuries are usually called physical, sexual, emotional, intellectual, verbal, or spiritual neglect or abuse. Most of this wounding neglect and abuse does not leave visible marks. And even when these hurts do result in physical signs, bruises soon fade and casts come off eventually. But the bloodless wounds and unseen soul-scars can last a lifetime.

This may seem like a melodramatic way of describing our human condition. And you may question whether my sweeping characterization of us and our interactions is warranted. That's fair. So I'll try to answer some of your major questions in these introductory pages.

First, what do hurt people who hurt people look like? Can you recognize them if they pass you on the sidewalk? Yes. And no. If they look like human beings, you've spotted one. The fact is that *all* of us are hurting people in either small or great ways.

On another level, the hurters' identities might shock us. For example, they may be startlingly young. Research shows that offenders under the age of eighteen commit over 70 percent of child abuse and assault.[1] Even more horrifying, there are increasing reports of children twelve and under molesting other children.

Overexposed to sexuality—promiscuity, pornography, incest, and sexualized violence—these perpetrator-victims no longer have the normal curiosity of young children. Said differently, sexually victimized young people are apt to sexually hurt other young people. And when we couch this children-molesting-children tragedy in the language of hurt people hurt people, we trace the answer to a second important question: How do hurt people hurt people?

When people try to function in areas that affect their untended wounds and unhealed hurts, they inevitably hurt others. Often they wound others as severely as they were hurt, and in remarkably similar ways. While most hurting is relatively mild, deeply wounded people deeply wound others.

Who do hurt people hurt? Usually those nearest and dearest to them. To be sure, strangers may superficially or profoundly wound us with their disrespectful rudeness, unprovoked violence, and so on. But our deepest wounds tend to come at the hands of those we love and trust.

Following my hurt-people-hurt-people premise, *we* too are most likely to wound those near and dear to *us*. This reality can trigger a serious case of the "if onlys." I've had repeated bouts of this life-crippling malady. My symptoms have included thoughts like this: "If only I could have met or seen my biological father—even once. If only he had wanted me instead of trying to abort me. If only my mom had sought help to improve her relationships with men, so I could have seen what a healthy family looked like. If only I had learned about the effects of my stepfather's alcoholism when I was younger so I could have been a better wife and mother. If only . . . if only."

But perhaps the most sweeping "if only" of all is this: if only hurt people did not hurt people. But they do. To one degree or another, people always have. They are doing so at this very moment. And *they* are *us*.

Pondering this reality that hurt people hurt people can leave us feeling pretty hopeless. And hopelessness can be deadly.

I once read about an elderly man in Detroit who shot himself after killing his wife. He was convinced he had contracted Lyme disease, though tests had come back negative. Guilt-stricken, thinking he had passed a deadly disease to his wife and seeing no hope for either of them, he concluded that murder and suicide were the only solution.[2]

Tragically, Lyme disease is neither contagious nor fatal. But the man's sense of hopelessness was.

When we hurt, we need hope to believe there really is some help for us to stop hurting—or at least to hurt less. I think you will find both help and hope in the following pages.

As you read, I invite you to pause, ponder, and pray about the sections that bother you most. Many readers benefit from keeping a journal of memories, thoughts, and feelings as they go. Remember, you will not go crazy or hurt someone just because you feel strong emotions. So why not give yourself permission to experience whatever emotions stir as you read?

Perhaps you've noticed that I've neglected to address the most troubling question: *Why* do hurt people hurt people? As strange as it may seem, part of the answer lies in the life-affirming aspect of our humanness that reflects the nature of our Creator.

> God is so devoted to life that He specializes in bringing life out of death.

He is for life! God is so devoted to life that He specializes in bringing life out of death. Jesus said that He came to bring us abundant and eternal life (John 10:10). He was even willing to die so that we could live forever with Him.

9

We all bear the image of God. This means that we all are for life. At the very least, you are for *your own* life. When we sense threats to our existence and well-being, we spontaneously act to protect and preserve our lives. It's normal to run, hide, even disguise our identity when we believe our lives are threatened. And we automatically flinch and protect a broken bone or raw physical wound when someone comes too close to it.

Similarly, in our sin-broken humanness, we normally adopt defensive, self-protective thinking and behavior patterns when we feel emotionally or relationally threatened and wounded.

This pattern would be different if we were perfect people. Perfect people would not hurt other people. Perfect people with perfect wisdom and faith would look to their loving Creator for protection and comfort.

As imperfect, sin-broken people, we are much more likely to trust in ourselves. So we inevitably and unknowingly choose lifestyles that make us feel more safe and comfortable. Inevitably, too, our lifestyles cause us more pain. And, as a side effect, they usually bring pain to others.

We don't stop being human when we start being Christian. This means that even after we have asked Jesus into our lives, we continue to struggle with the human trait of self-protection that leads us to hurt ourselves and others. Unseen emotional scars from wounds inflicted by others don't disappear any more than do visible, physical scars.

So when Christians experience painful suffering, emotional or physical, we are not strange spiritual misfits; we are human beings. And we are not backsliding or faithless if we seek human comfort and counsel when we hurt. Even the apostle Paul, one of Christianity's superstars, wasn't ashamed to admit he suffered physically and emotionally. And he wasn't shy about asking for comfort and help.

Near the end of his life, Paul was alone in a Roman prison—except for his friend Luke. Lonely, dreading the physical hardships of a cold winter ahead, and desiring physical and emotional warmth, Paul asked young Timothy to visit him with the comfort of a cloak and some companionship (2 Timothy 4:9, 21).

This is the same Paul who, under the Holy Spirit's guidance some years earlier, wrote that he could do all things through Christ's strength and told struggling believers that all their needs were met in the glorious riches of Christ (Philippians 4:13, 19). Those timeless truths did not change the fact that Paul was still human, needy, and sometimes lonely and hurting.

We see his humanity later when Paul describes himself as physically exhausted and fearful, while still giving thanks to God "who comforts the downcast" (2 Corinthians 7:6). In that particular circumstance, God chose to use a human vessel, Titus, to comfort Paul.

Our death-conquering Savior clearly and repeatedly modeled God's inclusion of human "co-workers" in His mission to bring life to others (1 Corinthians 3:9). As one example, in John 11 we see Jesus inviting concerned bystanders to participate in a death-to-life drama by telling them to move the stone from Lazarus's tomb and then instructing them to unwrap Lazarus's graveclothes. In between those two activities, Jesus spoke life into Lazarus's already decomposing body. Jesus directed human helpers to do what they could while He did what He alone could do—bring life out of death.

Sadly, some Christian leaders teach that experiencing pain and neediness is always a symptom of unconfessed sin or self-centeredness, and that seeking human help means distrusting the sufficiency of God's power.

Jesus Christ is the only all-sufficient and perfect healer for hurt people. And Jesus also graciously and frequently uses human instruments in His healing work. I am praying that our loving Lord Jesus will use this book as part of that process in your life.

PART 1
OUR HURTS

CHAPTER ONE

UNSEEN WOUNDS

"Here are four simple words that I call Wilson's Law of Relationships."

I have spoken that sentence at dozens of conferences and seminars across the United States, and the audience response is similar wherever I go. People smile or chuckle as they scribble my grandiose title in their notes. Then they look up expectantly to learn what comes next.

I continue, "Wilson's Law of Relationships says, 'Hurt people hurt people.'"

Suddenly smiles droop. Chuckles stop. A hush settles over the audience as many nod their heads and glance knowingly at companions.

I can relate to their responses because I am one of those hurt people who has hurt people. In fact, almost everyone I know identifies with the notion that hurt people hurt people. However, I've noticed a curious phenomenon: even when we see the result of this hurting and hurtful pattern in ourselves and others, we resist the idea that unseen injuries are real.

As I've listened to others and searched my own heart, I've concluded that many of our struggles spring from a belief that adults—especially Christian adults—should be beyond or above being hurt.

Are Good Christians "Wound-Proof"?

"If I were really a strong Christian, this wouldn't hurt so much. I just wish I could trust God more."

I've heard words similar to those for years as I have counseled Christian men and women. These dear people are judging their responses to a panorama of painful experiences including job loss, betrayal by a mate, sexual abuse by a parent, and even the death of a parent, child, or spouse.

Some personalize the "this shouldn't bother me" theme by adding something like, "My folks always told me I was too sensitive." Or, "My husband [or wife] tells me I'm just a cry-baby." Or perhaps, "My pastor keeps encouraging me to have more faith." But the basic refrain remains: "I should be able to take anything, no matter how cruel and crushing, without feeling any distress." Reframed in terms of unseen wounds: "No matter how traumatic the event, I should not let it hurt me."

Where do intelligent adults get the idea that any human being ought to be able to take everything without feeling anything?

A large part of the answer, I believe, is found in what I call *binding shame*.

Binding Shame

Have you ever felt as if you were the only caterpillar in a butterfly world? Do you often feel as if you have to do twice as much to be half as good as others? That's binding shame.[1]

Shame is the soul-deep belief that something is horribly wrong with me that is not wrong with anyone else in the entire world. If I am bound by shame, I feel hopelessly, disgustingly different and worthless. I mean literally *worth less* than other people.

The shame I am describing has little or nothing to do with true moral guilt, or what I call *biblical shame*. Scripture clearly states that each of us is utterly ruined by sin and completely guilty before God. No one can be more ruined than "utterly" nor more guilty than "completely."

God sees each of us as equally and helplessly bound in sin and deserving of the death penalty. And God invites each of us equally and lovingly to accept His free and gracious offer of salvation. From God's perspective, no person or group of persons is disgustingly different or worth less than others.

So where did many of us—yes, me too—get a blatantly unbiblical concept of shame?

Somebody misled us when we were too young to read and understand the Bible or to accurately interpret the world around us. Actually, it was probably a whole lot of somebodies who likely believed the lie themselves. (Deceived deceivers are just as dangerous and hurtful as calculated deceivers—if not more so.)

As I see it, shame is rooted in the lie that human beings can and should be perfect. And being perfect includes taking anything—that is, enduring any circumstance without feeling anything but fine and without behaving any way except nice.

But because I am unable to be unfailingly fine and nice, I know I am imperfect. And because I know I'm not perfect, I view myself as hideously flawed. So when I make a mistake, I don't simply *make* a mistake; *I am* a mistake. That is shame's lie in a nutshell. And that lie becomes the lens through which we see every experience.

> When I make a mistake, I don't simply *make* a mistake; *I am* a mistake. That is shame's lie in a nutshell.

I don't understand why or how I got so hideously different; I just know that I've always been that way. It's like having an invisible, irreparable birth defect. So, of course, that means there is no chance to change. "That's just the way I am." Have you said that to yourself? Or perhaps you've heard it at a family gathering. "Don't make such a big deal out of Grandma's sharp tongue; that's just the way she is." Or, "Don't pay any attention to Uncle Jeff's dirty jokes; that's just part of his personality."

When I am bound by shame, it contaminates all my perceptions, choices, and relationships. What's more, the "I'm different and worthless" perspective leaves me feeling isolated from everyone around me. I believe that my only chance to connect with perfect people is either to convince them that I can fill a need in their life or to trick them into thinking that I too am perfect.

The relationship between binding shame and unseen wounds involves a curious malady: inner blindness. In other words, shame not only *binds* us but also *blinds* us—as I know only too well.

My Bout with Binding, Blinding Shame

When my mother married my father, she did not know that he was a bigamist and an embezzler, but he was. When he learned that my mother was pregnant with me, he tried repeatedly to prevent my birth by insisting that my mother abort me. When she refused, he tried to induce a miscarriage. When that failed, he tried several times to kill her (and me) in what would look like a gun-cleaning accident. Before he could succeed, God intervened, and federal authorities caught up with him and put him in prison.

Consequently, I've never met, seen, spoken to, or seen even a scrap of handwriting from my biological father.

Decades before single motherhood was seen as normal, my mother had a fatherless infant to care for in a place thousands of miles from family and friends.

At the hospital where I was born and where she worked as a physical therapist, rumors spread about my illegitimacy. Shortly before my mother's death, I got a deeper understanding of her shame and humiliation when she told me about putting her marriage license on the main hospital bulletin board to silence the rumors.

Two years later my mother married the alcoholic stepfather I believed was my birth father until she told me differently when I was ten. She divorced him three years later when his alcohol-related violence escalated to life-threatening levels.

I'm still missing chunks of my chaotic childhood. For nearly three decades, I erased the horror and humiliation of sexual molestation at the hands of a stranger, family "friends," and, the worst, a step-uncle.

How could those and many other awful experiences occur when I had an intelligent, well-educated, hardworking mom who loved me very much and loved God even more?

Part of the answer is that my mother herself was deeply wounded by shame. Her unseen wounds showed up most clearly in an inability to have a healthy, mutually respectful romantic relationship, resulting in five marriages to four husbands.

Living the Shame

Alcoholic families are fertile seedbeds for shame. As the oldest child and self-appointed hero, I tried to fix the family and make my mother happy by being a good—no, make that *perfect*—child. Naturally, I failed. Naturally, too, I blamed myself for not being good enough to do the impossible.

In addition, my shame-bound mother looked to her children to mend her tattered self-concept. As a result, she conveyed to us that achievements that reflected well on her were what made us valuable. This early emphasis launched me into a lifetime of perfectionistic performance and other people-pleasing behaviors to earn approval and love.

How did I cope as an imperfect and hurting person who believed I should be perfect? I became a self-protective perfectionist and approval addict, clueless as to what was going on inside me. The shame that was binding me also was blinding me.

Unbiblical shame comes bound with a kind of "existence guilt" when we believe that only perfect people deserve life and happiness. To see and acknowledge our imperfections seems life-threatening, so we close our eyes to them. We are afraid to risk the honest self-examination necessary for integrity and wholeness. At least, that's how I functioned most of my life.

> **Unbiblical shame comes bound with a kind of "existence guilt" when we believe that only perfect people deserve life and happiness.**

All of this was true even though I loved God and believed in Him. However, *what* I believed about God added to my heavy load of shame instead of lifting it.

A God Who Cares about Our Inner Lives

Like many other sincere but shame-shackled Christians, I had distorted the God of the Bible from being the God who "looks at the heart" (1 Samuel 16:7) into a god who looks at outward appearance. After all, serving a deity who focuses on the external observance of religious rituals seems appealingly familiar and doable to those of us already caught up in performance-based living.

Whether or not we realize it, we all read and interpret the Bible through the defective lens of personal experience. Not surprisingly, the deity we see has views that are amazingly similar to our own!

I pulled off that convenient and comforting theological sleight of hand for most of my life. However, God kept insisting that I get to know Him as He really is and then allow Him to be Himself.

God places a very high value on truth. Jesus, in fact, called Himself truth (John 14:6). And unlike humans who typically emphasize externals, God focuses primarily on our unseen, inner lives—or, as Scripture usually terms it, our hearts. Proverbs 4:23 tells us to guard our hearts because our external lives flow out of our internal selves. Jesus echoed this concept when He declared that all our visible behaviors spill out of our unseen inner lives—again, our "heart" (Mark 7:21).

So it's no surprise that the God of truth who looks primarily at our hearts calls us to live in total truth—truth inside, which only He sees, and truth outside, which others see. Yet many believers are unfamiliar with God's desire for us to have "truth in [our] innermost being" (Psalm 51:6 NASB).

> **The God of truth who looks primarily at our hearts calls us to live in total truth—truth inside, which only He sees, and truth outside, which others see.**

Consider this: The apostle Paul tells Christians to "examine" themselves before they participate in the Lord's Supper (1 Corinthians 11:28). As I understand this process, it includes looking inwardly at the condition of our hearts as truthfully as possible and then looking to Jesus in faith to forgive the sin we discover.

Prolonged unforgiveness, murderous rage, and adulterous thoughts are examples of sins we might find during an inner examination. These are just a few of the hurtful ways we respond to unseen emotional and relational wounds. But we are unlikely to let God give us wisdom in the hidden parts of our hearts when we believe He wants us to keep ignoring that inside stuff.

If we were to follow that line of reasoning, we would come to the conclusion that God sanctions, indeed sanctifies, what I call *anointed amnesia*—that is, the denial of reality. However,

God is calling us out of dark, dank caves of denial into the honest risk of truth's light.

Scripture says that we will not "prosper" if we conceal our sins instead of admitting them and seeking forgiveness (Proverbs 28:13). Perhaps the same principle applies to inner wounds when we continue to hide them rather than seek healing.

When we hide from painful truths, we deprive ourselves of discovering that Jesus, the Great Physician, is as able to heal our unseen wounds as He is to forgive our sins.

Pause to Ponder and Pray

Ponder

Read the following verses in more than one translation of the Bible. You will discover that God cares a lot more about our inner selves and our hidden wounds than most of us realize. Clearly, God calls us to greater self-awareness so that we can relinquish the defensive self-absorption that often marks the lives of us hurt people.

- Proverbs 4:23. Compare with Mark 7:21. Note that the "heart" (thoughts, will, etc.) is the source of everything others see and know about us.
- 1 Samuel 16:7. Note that God looks on our hearts. He goes to the source of who we are.
- Psalm 51:6. God wants us to have truth at the source. He promises to give us wisdom in the inner parts—the parts that are hidden from our awareness.

Pray

> *Lord, it's scary to think about leaving*
> *familiar hiding places. Help me to love*

22

*truthful self-awareness more than fearful
self-absorption. And please help me know the
difference. Make me willing to commit to you
my thoughts, feelings, and memories. Amen.*

CHAPTER TWO

THE PROBLEM OF UNSEEN WOUNDS

You could see the tragedy coming in the lengthening shadows of early evening as the adorable five-year-old dashed into the street after her soccer ball. The approaching car squealed its brakes, but to no avail. There was a dull thud, a driver's horrified gasp, and a crumpled body covered with blood.

The girl's mother rushed out, screaming, "Sophie, Sophie. Oh, my girl." The driver sobbed as he bent over the delicate body. Sophie's dad yelled for onrushing neighbors to call an ambulance. Within minutes the emergency squad arrived and whisked the injured child to the nearest emergency room. Soon she was in surgery to repair her damaged limbs.

During the following weeks in the hospital, Sophie received dozens of cards, gifts, and visits. The outpouring of loving concern continued during her lengthy recovery at home. And long after Sophie could walk without limping, neighbors and church friends asked how she was feeling and assured her that they were still praying for her.

Another little girl dashed into the street. She too was struck by a car. Another dull thud was heard as flesh collided with metal. Another crumpled child lay covered with blood. But that's where the similarity ended.

Not only did the driver fail to stop, but he didn't even glance back to see what he hit. Margaret's parents did not rush out. Neighbors and emergency personnel did not aid her. In fact, as unbelievable as it sounds, no one even noticed. When Margaret recovered consciousness, she slowly dragged her battered, bloodied body into the house. Somehow she crawled into the bathroom and cleaned herself as well as she could while her family members continued their tasks as if nothing out of the ordinary had happened.

When Margaret dragged herself to the table for supper, her mother yelled at her for walking funny. Her father ordered her to "wipe that stupid look" off her face. Neither parent acknowledged her bruises, bent limbs, and the dried blood on the back of her head.

Imagine if that incredibly painful experience happened to Margaret over and over again. Imagine what it would be like for Margaret if the driver of the car were her father or someone else she loved and trusted.

Believe it or not, there are Margarets all around us. I saw them in my counseling office for years. They are women and men who are deeply wounded, and although their injuries are invisible, their pain is real.

If it's true that hurt people hurt people, we have a major problem. By ignoring so many hurting people because their injuries remain invisible to us, we are creating a new generation of hurtful people. When pain is real, the wounds are also real, even if they remain unseen.

Unseen Does Not Mean Unreal

"No tears unless you're bleeding!"

One daughter recalls this phrase as her father's most memorable words. Sadly, such a rule reinforces one of the major problems of unseen wounds: *because they are unseen, no one believes they are real.*

> **Broken bones mend. Black eyes fade. But the unseen wounds and invisible scars of emotional battering remain.**

Broken bones mend. Black eyes fade. But the unseen wounds and invisible scars of emotional battering remain. And they create emergencies as serious as broken arms and fractured skulls.

Many doubt the reality of wounds unless a person can display scars from physical abuse. Others may accept the reality of unseen wounds if they cause some type of physiological malfunction. One lovely Christian woman I know was left permanently sterile when her parents performed a coat-hanger abortion after she was impregnated by her father. She was fourteen at the time.

We have no trouble accepting the fact that this woman has permanent damage in her uterus. Why are we surprised that she also has scars in her relational, spiritual, and personal life? Why is it hard to believe that these emotional scars inhibit her sexual relationship with her husband? And why should we be amazed that similar dynamics are operating in our own lives even though the original wounds and their present expressions are entirely different?

Many sincere Christians might think, "That's just self-justification, self-centeredness, and sin. Tell her to pray, read her Bible more, and snap out of it." Most of them do not say it quite so directly, but I've encountered many who believe it.

Excuse for Sin or Context for Change?

As someone who deeply loves God and His Word, I do not deny the reality of personal sin and its consequences when I affirm the reality of unseen wounds and their effects. Without doubt, Scripture declares that the primary wound affecting all of us is spiritual. And it is self-inflicted. Our original parents set the sorry

26

cycle in motion in Eden by trusting their own wisdom and ways instead of their Creator's, whose image they bore (see Genesis 3).

God did not remove from us His image—that is, the spiritual, rational, emotional, and relational aspects of His character that He imparted to humans at creation. But when the original image bearers fell, every aspect of God's image in them was shattered beyond recognition.

According to the Bible, each of us has subsequently followed the same self-destructive path. This defection from our created condition triggered a complete disabling of every aspect of our humanness. In the physical realm, human bodies are vulnerable to damage from machines, microbes, and many other sources. In the mental realm, the detrimental effects of sin can be seen in the flaws and fallacies of human reasoning. None of us are exempt from this sin-scar on our thought lives, and this reality is the reason God tells us to seek wisdom from Him rather than rely on our own or another human's imperfect understanding (Psalm 118:8; Proverbs 3:5).

This is an important concept, because it shows that we accept the reality of damaged thinking processes even though we cannot see the injuries, wounds, and sin-related irregularities. We believe they exist because we see their effects. For example, when I rationally weigh the facts and logically conclude that my ideas are almost always right and that my exceedingly bright husband's views are almost always wrong, I am seeing my sin-damaged thinking in all its self-serving glory, whether I recognize it or not!

So far, I've offered evidence that sin damages us physically and intellectually. But we are more than bodies and brains, and we can be wounded in other areas as well.

Emotional and Relational Natures and Wounds

The Bible portrays God as having powerful emotions. We see His emotional nature expressed most clearly in God the Son.

Jesus was "full of joy" at the good report of the seventy-two disciples He had sent out to announce the coming kingdom of God (Luke 10:21), and He wept at the grave of his friend Lazarus (John 11:35). Jesus also was "overwhelmed with sorrow" in Gethsemane (Matthew 26:38) and felt intense anger (John 2:14–17). And Jesus loved. He loved His disciples. He loved Lazarus and his sisters, who returned His affection, and He loved the rich young ruler, who did not (Mark 10:17–22).

God is not only a rational and emotional being; God is also relational. We see this in the triune Godhead—Father, Son, and Holy Spirit. God's emotional and relational characteristics are significant elements in the sin-shattered image we still bear. So why do we expect our brokenness to be different in emotional and relational areas than in the physical and intellectual realms?

> **God is not only a rational and emotional being; God is also relational.**

In my experience, the folks who resist this concept most are those who are most uncomfortable with their emotions.

If we draw a physical analogy to minimizing or denying human emotions and our vulnerability to emotional hurt, it might sound something like this: "Bodies are bothersome and potentially dangerous. It's better for me if I don't have a body so it can't be hurt and it can't hurt others. So I'll just pretend my body doesn't exist. If that fails, I'll deaden my body so it can't ever feel any pain. After all, when I feel pain, I'm reminded that my body is real. And if it's real, I'd need to know how to keep it healthy."

Clearly, such statements are unbiblical and unhelpful for anyone facing physical distress. This holds for situations of *emotional* distress too.

My efforts to cast emotional struggles in a physical-suffering mold in no way excuses injured people from taking responsibility for their choices and their lives. This becomes clearer when we understand the process involved in recovering from physical injuries.

The Physical Therapy Model

When it comes to physical injuries, patients are responsible to participate with their therapists in the healing process. This is true whether the injuries were inflicted accidentally or intentionally, whether by the patient or by others.

Furthermore, patients often are given homework of painful stretching and exercise because caregivers realize that healing doesn't magically occur in the presence of medical personnel within white-walled rooms.

When we acknowledge physical injuries and seek help, no one accuses us of trying to escape personal responsibility; we are simply accepting the truth that we live in a fallen world where sin affects all people. What's more, we are still responsible for what we do about our injuries. And recognizing the nature and extent of our wounds provides a helpful context for working toward changes that bring greater wholeness.

> Rather than acknowledging the existence of our invisible inner injuries and treating them, we often attempt to distance ourselves from them.

What I Can't See Can Hurt Me (and Others)

When we seek to numb the pain of unseen wounds—either knowingly or unknowingly—with denial or other emotional anesthetics, we inevitably create additional pain for ourselves and for others. Rather than acknowledging the existence of our invisible inner injuries and treating them, we often attempt to distance ourselves from them by deflecting our pain onto those around us. And, typically, we hurt *others* most deeply in the areas of *our* deepest wounding.

Annie has been on the receiving end of this principle. This is how she described being hurt by deflected pain.

> My husband, Joe, and I have never made a secret of the fact that the Lord gave us Addy through the efforts of a Christian lawyer in a private adoption. Everybody in Joe's family and mine knows and understands and is happy for us. We tried for nine years to get pregnant. We didn't consider adoption until after all that time, tens of thousands of dollars in medical procedures, and seeking God's will with our pastor and our Bible study group praying for us. You can't imagine how shocked Joe and I were when his cousin called us "black market baby buyers" in front of his entire family at the Christmas open house.
>
> I was speechless and so was Joe. I mumbled something about everything being done legally and left the room as quickly as possible. Later, Joe's mom told me that, at seventeen, this un-married cousin had given up a baby girl for adoption. I felt really sorry for her and was really glad she made the choice she did instead of having an abortion. But I was still crushed by what she said, and because she said it in front of the whole family.

Learning to see that this cousin was hurting, not just hurtful, helped Annie and Joe forgive and eventually reach out to her in love.

Hurt people commonly use anger to disguise and deflect their guilt and grief just as Joe's cousin did. Anger provides an illusion of personal power that temporarily blocks feelings of confusion and helplessness that often result from painful crises. Although this unfairly hurts others, there are even more devastating ways of trying to numb pain from unseen wounds.

When Victims Become Victimizers

Numerous studies have uncovered a strong relationship between abuse experienced in childhood and adult abuse potential.[1] This statement sounds dry and dispassionate, but if we bend our ears to listen to its heartbeat, we hear the unmistakable roar of throbbing pain.

The reasoning behind this seems to follow this logic: If I overpower, dominate, and abuse you today, it temporarily numbs the pain I still have because I was overpowered, dominated, and abused yesterday. Apparently victims gain a sense of inner strength and personal mastery by dominating someone even more powerless than themselves.

When we trace the roots of emotional pain back to the source, it can fuzz the lines between victim and victimizer to the point that we miss a crucial truth: *understanding a behavior does not make it acceptable.*

Sometimes I use this reminder to pull me out of the quicksand of sympathy and set me firmly on the rock of personal responsibility. The alternative is to surrender and say that no one can reverse the intergenerational cycle. If that is true, the only comfort for today's victims is the assurance that their turn to be victimizers is coming soon. Surely there is something better.

God has a name for that something better. He calls it wisdom. Scripture says that "prudent" people give thought to their "ways"—that is, their manner of living (Proverbs 14:8). This mindset is contrasted with that of the foolish, who are characterized by deception. Deception flows in two directions: inward and outward, as we try to convince ourselves and others that we are strong and invincible instead of weak, wounded, and easily hurt.

Psalm 139:23–24 tells us how self-deceptive people like us can understand the true nature of our lives. The psalmist, in seeking the truth about himself, asked God to search his heart to see if there was any "hurtful" way within him (NASB). Some translations use the word "wicked" (NKJV) or "offensive" (NIV) instead. All three translations describe a manner of living that is potentially harmful to oneself and others.

I haven't always had the psalmist's courage. How about you? When we lack understanding about our hurtful ways, we cannot make healthy, hurt-free choices. And so the cycle of hurt and pain rolls on.

Pause to Ponder and Pray

Ponder

- Have you been the target of a comment like the one made by Joe's cousin? If so, who made it? Did you ever find out why they made the comment?

- Have you ever made such a comment yourself? To whom?

- Take a moment to write a response that would more accurately reflect God's perspective on the subject of inner wounds—your own or someone else's. (Review Proverbs 18:14.)

- Do you think you may be wounding others because you haven't been willing to own your wounds? If so, who are you wounding? How are you doing it?

Pray

> *Lord, please continue to teach me to value self-awareness and inner honesty as much as your Word reveals that you do. And give me the wisdom to know if today is one of those times when I need to pay special attention to the wounds I can't see—especially those that wound people close to me. Amen.*

CHAPTER THREE

HURT BY THE UNPREPARED AND UNAVAILABLE

As my husband was driving me home from the hospital with our three-day-old firstborn, he glanced over and uttered these unforgettable words: "Do you know anything about taking care of a baby?"

Trying to muster an expression of indignation, I replied, "Of course."

I lied.

Most people receive more instruction for driving a car than for becoming a parent, and we were no exception. No wonder even the most loving parents flounder and fail from time to time.

"They did the best they could" is a phrase often used in reference to parents. It is more truthful to say that parents do the best they *know*, and no one knows how to be a consistently good parent. Even the most well-meaning parents unintentionally inflict hurts by being unprepared, unavailable, or, more likely, a combination of both.

In parenting—as in other areas of life—we can do little to prepare for the unexpected, other than expect it. The truth is, parenting has more "expecteds" than "unexpecteds." The study of child development has confirmed that children develop in predictable ways at predictable times. Parents who do not understand normal child development often hurt their children unintentionally. This contributes to unnecessary and undeserved shame in the child.

Reinforcing Biological Shame

Children are physically and intellectually different from and less than parents and other adults. Some children come to believe that this condition is permanent. Those who do assume that they are condemned to spend their entire lives never knowing how to solve the mysteries of muddy feet or multiplication tables. This is what I call *biological shame*. Whereas binding shame is a sense of being different from and worth less than other people, biological shame is a sense of being different from and worth less than adults.[1]

Because the basis of biological shame is a temporary condition, the cure is one-hundred-percent effective. It's called aging. At some point, children become equal in height, strength, skill, and intelligence to the adults they considered geniuses.

If, in the normal course of maturing, children outgrow the basis for biological shame, how does it do damage? The answer lies in hurtful parental responses to normal developmental limitations.

Here are examples of hurtful versus helpful parental responses to expectable childhood behavior: a three-year-old's inability to keep pace with a parent when shopping.

Hurtful and Shaming Response: "Hey, slowpoke, why can't you keep up with me?" "Watch out, clumsy. You bumped into that lady's grocery cart." "Stop wandering off all over the place. I haven't got all day to spend looking for you."

Helpful and Non-shaming Response: "You look like you're almost running to stay up with me. My legs are a lot longer than yours because I'm grown-up, so I'd better slow down a little. I remember how hard it was for me to keep up with my mommy and daddy. Oops, we need to look out for the carts."

You get the idea. Children naturally walk more slowly, are less coordinated, and are more easily distracted than adults. These expectable limitations disappear in time, and they need not be a source of shame for children. For parents who understand and adapt their expectations to child development patterns, they won't be. In contrast, unprepared parents who have unrealistic developmental expectations will shame their children for not fulfilling them.

> **Unprepared parents who have unrealistic developmental expectations will shame their children for not fulfilling them.**

Unless developmental difficulties occur, children one day will end up on the adult side of life. Sadly, some of these adult children will be scarred by the hurts inflicted by loving but unprepared parents who held unrealistic developmental expectations.

What's true about unrealistic physical development expectations usually carries over to intellectual and skill development expectations as well. I know of an eight-year-old girl who was harshly criticized—ridiculed, actually—for not knowing how to follow a recipe. A ten-year-old boy received a similar parental response for not trimming hedges correctly. No adult had taken the time to teach these children how to accomplish their assigned tasks, but both were expected to perform perfectly.

Patient, persistent skill-building instruction takes time and energy. When parents are distracted by their own unhealed wounds, the pain demands all their attention and drains the emotional energy needed to instruct children. And distracted parents are unavailable parents.

Hands-Off Hurts from Unavailable Parents

I had two unavailable fathers. The first, my biological father, was unavailable because of deception. The second, my stepdad, was unavailable because of alcoholism and divorce. But you don't have to come from a single-parent family to know what it's like to be hurt by unavailable parents. In addition to divorce, desertion, and death, parents' personal problems and poor priorities can create emotional orphans.

Hurt by Parents with Personal Problems

"Long-term cognitive, psychological, and health outcomes associated with child abuse and neglect," a recent study title proclaimed. Along with blatant acts of sexual and physical abuse, the article listed a form of parental treatment that is a risk factor for cognitive and educational delays, unhealthy sexual relationships, drug use, and experiencing harassment later in life. "In conclusion, child maltreatment, particularly emotional abuse and neglect, is associated with a wide range of long-term adverse health and developmental outcomes."[2]

If that sounds overstated, you will be surprised to learn that this research is actually old news. Even Job knew about unavailable parents:

> If their children are honored, they do not
> know it;
> if their offspring are brought low, they do
> not see it.
> They feel but the pain of their own bodies
> and mourn only for themselves.
> (Job 14:21–22)

What an extraordinary statement about emotionally unavailable parents! Distracted by personal pain, they notice neither their children's achievements nor their afflictions.

You may be unable to relate to weak, needy, depressed, or despondent parents. Your folks may have been successful, high energy, go-get-'em kinds of people. If so, don't be surprised to discover that you also may have hands-off hurts.

Hurt by Parents with Poor Priorities

Some of us grew up in families where parents were nearly always too busy, too tired, or too important to be available.

This pattern is common in the homes of pastors, missionaries, denominational leaders, seminary professors, parachurch personnel, and other ministry types—including therapists, speakers, and authors.

Jeff spoke like an authority on this subject.

"Did you ever think of the phone as a lethal weapon?" he asked, his intense brown eyes searching my face for a reply.

Before I could offer one, he continued.

"I grew up dreading the sound of the phone because every time it rang, it meant death to any hope of spending time with my folks—especially my dad. He wasn't a bad guy at all. In fact, everyone in our town thought he was great. He was a successful real estate broker, an elder at church, and the leader of the local branch of a well-known Christian organization. It's just that he never had time to do stuff with me, you know—stuff like go to my soccer games or really talk to me. I mean really talk."

> **Parents are just as likely to wound children in their areas of success as in their area of suffering.**

Jeff's experience is neither new nor unique. In fact, the kind of family Jeff described is epidemic in our hurried, harried, pressure-cooker society—and also in our society-pressured churches. Parents are just as likely to wound children in their areas of success as in their area of suffering.

Families exist to meet genuine human needs. One of the most important of these needs is the nurturing of children. This God-designed enterprise requires a major investment of time and attention. However, many successful people treat their children like inconvenient impediments to be dispatched in as little time and with as little attention as possible. This approach frees the parents so they can move to the next item on their list of important things.

No doubt the majority of these unavailable, overscheduled parents would raise a chorus of "But I never meant to hurt my kids." So why do they continue doing just that? The answer lies in the fact that these and all parents function as mirrors to their children—mirrors with messages.

Messages from Marred Mirrors

As children, we believed that the image of ourselves that we saw mirrored in our parents' faces and in their behavior toward us accurately reflected our true identities.

This is why our self-image fundamentally is a mirror image. In effect, all children live in Snow White's zip code.

"Mirror, mirror, on the wall, who's the fairest of them all?" The evil queen in *Snow White* knew she would always hear the truth when the talking magical mirror answered her question. Children possess a talking mirror of their own. It's called Mommy and Daddy. And children assume that talking mirrors always tell the truth. That's why they accept without question the reflection they see of themselves in their parents' faces.

> **Young children lack the reasoning skills to figure out that what they see in their parents' faces and hear in their parents' voices reflects and echoes who the *parent* is, not who the *child* is.**

Young children lack the reasoning skills to figure out that what they see in their parents' faces and hear in their parents' voices reflects and echoes who the *parent* is, not who the *child* is. Children have no way of knowing that even the most loving parents are marred mirrors. Most flaws are due to inadequate preparation, poor priorities, and personal problems. What's more, all parents are wounded to some degree by their own hurting and hurtful parents. As a result, parents may unintentionally send confusing and distressing messages to their children.

Listening to the Messages We Received

In hurtful families, normal childhood behavior elicits wounding responses from parents with unrealistic expectations and perfectionistic demands. These wounding responses send loud, clear identity messages to their children. In effect, a child's imperfect and awkward or inappropriate behavior becomes a definitive statement about that child's identity and worth.

The following chart displays several examples of typical childhood behavior and includes helpful and hurtful parental responses along with the identity messages children likely hear from each response. As you read them, recall your own childhood and ask yourself which statements sound most familiar.

Contrasting Parental Responses and the Messages They Send

Helpful Response	Message	Hurtful Response	Message
Situation: Three-year-old is wriggling in restaurant booster chair			
"Look at the pretty crayons they gave you. Here, you can color on your place mat."	My parents like me and they help me find interesting things to do.	"Stop that wriggling. Sit up straight. How many times do we have to tell you to behave yourself, you little brat!"	I can't be the way I should be. I don't make my parents happy. I am a brat.

Helpful Response	Message	Hurtful Response	Message
Situation: Kindergartner spills a glass of milk at breakfast			
"Oh dear, there goes the milk. Paper towels will soak that up in a jiffy. I must have filled your glass too full."	Paper towels are good for cleaning up spilled milk.	"Oh great, as if I didn't have enough to do. You are always so clumsy and careless. What a mess!"	I am a clumsy and careless person. I make messes and am a lot of bother to people.
Situation: Fourth grader leaves art project on dining table			
"I need you to clean up your project so I can set the table. Let's see if we can find a special place for it to dry."	I am expected to clean up after myself. My interests are important.	"You are always such a selfish slob. Just look at all the junk you left in here."	I am a selfish slob. My interests and things are junk.
Situation: Ten-year-old reminds Dad about Little League game			
"I wouldn't miss it! You really look like you're having a great time with the team this year. Am I right?"	My dad thinks I'm important. He wants me to enjoy myself when I play baseball.	"Yeah, well, I know I promised to come, but I'm just too busy with this project. All you do is strike out anyway."	I am bad to want my dad to come to my games. I am not as important as his work. I am not good enough to earn his attention.

The first two examples of hurtful responses are from parents who react inappropriately because they don't recognize age-appropriate behavior. They expect their children to behave as if they are older than they are. These children receive a command that is impossible to obey: be someone other than who you are. That's a lot like saying to a brown-eyed child, "Make your eyes blue and then I'll listen to you."

Impossible-to-satisfy expectations end up as hurtful messages for children who receive them. When children consume a steady diet of wounding messages, they come to believe that some soul-deep, fundamental flaw dooms them to a lifetime of failure.

The second two examples of hurtful responses are from parents who have poor priorities. Parents need to be available to their children to help them find room and time for their activities and interests. But when dads or moms are too preoccupied with projects at home or at the office, they are unavailable to their children.

Unavailable Parents Mean Unmet Needs

All children need the emotional security and nurturing that come from a safe, gentle embrace. They also need parental attention and companionship. When parents are unavailable because of personal problems or poor priorities, they may want to—even promise to—meet their children's needs, sincerely intending to do just that. But these unavailable parents are unlikely to follow through on their pledges.

> Children with parents who consistently treat needs, interests, and feelings as unimportant and unworthy of time and attention learn to see themselves as unimportant and unworthy of care.

Feeling the void of unmet needs and the string of broken promises, children begin to believe that there is something wrong with their needs. They are unable to understand that there is something wrong instead with their parents' commitment to promises.

As a result, children with parents who consistently treat needs, interests, and feelings as unimportant and unworthy of time and attention learn to see themselves as unimportant and unworthy of care. Confronted with such a deeply wounding situation, many determine to somehow become good enough to be noticed and loved.

Bill developed an interest in bodybuilding to make his dad proud of him. Bill's father was quite the successful athlete, and he expected no less of his sons. But Bill was a big disappointment. He was not well coordinated and did not excel at any sport like his older brothers did. So Bill began lifting weights. It didn't require as much coordination—just a lot of determination and hard work. And steroids produced amazing results.

At the time I saw Bill's story on television, he had been off steroids about a year because of severe liver and kidney damage. When the interviewer asked why he kept using steroids after knowing about their damaging side effects, Bill said he had to because he wanted to win at higher and higher levels of competition.

"Winning was that important to you?" the surprised reporter asked. "So important that you'd risk your health?"

"Well, I guess it does sound crazy," Bill answered. "But I just kept hoping that if I won a more important competition, it would make my dad proud of me."

At the end of the segment, the reporter asked Bill if his father was proud of his bodybuilding achievements.

Bill replied, "My dad never saw me compete."

I wish I could talk to Bill and tell him that it's fine to compete for bodybuilding titles, but no child—Bill or any other—was meant to compete for a parent's love.

Pause to Ponder and Pray

Ponder

Complete the following to help you hear your "talking mirrors." Remember, most parents love their children and do the best they know how to do.

As a child, I was good when _____.

As a child, I was bad when _____.

Pray

> *Lord, help me to remember that my parents were imperfect, hurting people just like me. Remind me that lying is not loving, and help me be willing to seek truth more than approval. Amen.*

CHAPTER FOUR

HURT BY LIARS AND THIEVES

To one degree or another, all parents are hurting people. And to one degree or another, all parents are hurting other people, most likely the tiny, helpless, trusting people born into their families.

Most parents work hard to provide loving, appropriate care for their children. Other parents miss that mark because they are unprepared or unavailable. But parents who neglect and abuse their children are, in fact, liars and thieves.

Parents function as liars and thieves for many reasons that all have a common denominator: personal sin expressed as unresolved, life-dominating problems. The problems might be from chemical dependency or from emotional instability like chronic, untreated depression or rage. However, the results are the same for the children: fear, confusion, distrust, anger, insecurity, and the list goes on.

Parents create the first universe that young children inhabit. In healthy families, this universe is a secure and stable place where the bigger, more knowledgeable citizens truthfully answer the questions and meet the needs of the smaller, less sophisticated inhabitants.

Parents Who Steal from Children

Apart from unavoidable financial crisis, parents provide the family's basic needs of food, shelter, and clothing. This means that in well-functioning families, children can expect to live under a roof where they receive food to keep them healthy and clothes to keep them covered and protected.

God takes parental responsibility very seriously. In the apostle Paul's first letter to the young church leader Timothy, he wrote, "Anyone who does not provide for their relatives, and especially for their own household, has denied the faith and is worse than an unbeliever" (1 Timothy 5:8).

That's pretty strong language. Unfortunately, some impaired parents re-order family priorities with weird and wounding results.

> When parents elevate pleasure, convenience, wealth, their own safety, or other things above the basic material needs of their children, their children get the message not only that they *get* nothing but also that they *are* nothing.

Stealing Security

Ted was raised on a farm where his father, a prominent authority on agriculture and animal husbandry, fed his show animals better than his sons and daughters. Ted remembers fighting over a piece of fruit with his sisters and brother while the feeding troughs in the barn overflowed.

Decades later Ted learned that his father paid twice the usual employee contribution into his company's retirement program, leaving inadequate resources to meet the basic needs of his wife and children. Ironically, and perhaps justly, Ted's father died before retirement age and never enjoyed one penny of his doubly endowed retirement fund.

Parents who focus on their own needs to the detriment of their children are a hallmark of unhealthy families. When parents elevate pleasure, convenience, wealth, their own safety, or other things above the basic material needs of their children, their children get the message not only that they *get* nothing but also that they *are* nothing.

Just as the provision of basic material needs establishes an atmosphere of security in a family, the performance of leadership roles provides a sense of stability. Sadly, impaired parents routinely abdicate leadership in their hurting and hurtful families.

Stealing Stability

As parents age, some reversal of the parent-child role is unavoidable. However, when irresponsible and immature parents abdicate the leadership role in the family to their young and adolescent children, not only is it avoidable; it is inexcusable.

"I was so terrified!" That's how Jenn described feeling at age six when she had to snatch her baby brother out of his crib, call the fire department, and try to drag and shove her tranquilized mother out of the house after she had fallen asleep with a cigarette in her hand.

In less dramatic cases, children of seven or eight or even younger frequently cook for themselves and their younger siblings, wash their own clothes, and try to parent themselves while their parents are preoccupied with jobs, affairs, depression, legal or illegal substances, church activities, or some combination of the above.

This kind of upside-down family is frightening not only to the child-parent in charge but also to the siblings. Younger children figure out early that kids (even older kids) are not intended to be—or adequate to be—parents. When young children discover that their security is in jeopardy because family stability rests in the shaky hands of irresponsible parents or the tiny hands of other children, they instinctively become focused on staying alive by keeping themselves safe.

In contrast, in a home where parents provide a secure, stable environment, children are free to explore and enjoy the safe universe their parents create. To assume that those in more secure, stable families are going to develop in healthier ways does not require much of a stretch. After all, keeping oneself safe drains a lot of energy that could go into developing creativity and healthy confidence. Since safety is our most basic need, safety ought to be a given in families. Sadly, it is not.

Stealing Safety

I grow weary of reading news articles and weeping over stories I've heard from counseling clients and seminar attendees of horrendous, often unspeakable physical and sexual abuse suffered at the hands of parents, grandparents, and other family caregivers. My file of child abuse cases is bulging, my heart is breaking, and there is no end in sight.

My husband uses the term *no-brainer* for situations that are so obvious that they don't require any expenditure of mental energy to explain or understand. Surely, it ought to be a no-brainer to expect children's arms, legs, and genitals to be safe in their own homes. Oh, how I wish it were.

Stealing Physical Safety. Some thieves of childhood safety are blatant about it. Here are some of the ways they steal physical safety:

- Slapping, shaking, scratching, sticking with pins
- Squeezing tight enough to cause pain, hitting or beating with such things as boards, sticks, belts, kitchen utensils, yardsticks, electrical cords, hoses, shovels
- Burning, scalding, freezing, holding under water
- Throwing, pushing, shoving, or slamming against walls, floors, or objects

- Confining in closets, basements, attics, boxes, locked rooms
- Withholding food or water[1]

Unfortunately, this list is representative, not exhaustive.

Some parents steal safety in a subtle way called *vicarious abuse.* This term acknowledges the reality that when a person witnesses anyone else being abused, he or she is also a victim of that abuse. This is true especially for children. When a pet, piece of furniture, or even a part of a house receives a violent blow, children fear that they will be at the receiving end of the next punch.

Another subtle type of hands-off physical child abuse is verbal violence.

In verbally violent families, kids grow up hearing statements like, "If you say another word, I'll cram my fist down your throat." Young children often become very anxious about how to protect themselves since they have no way of knowing when such threats might become reality. A verbally violent family may never come to physical blows, yet such a family steals a child's sense of safety by creating an atmosphere of impending harm.

Physical safety is not the only casualty in unhealthy families. Some parents also steal sexual safety and, in the process, slay sexual innocence.

Stealing Sexual Safety and Innocence. Estimates suggest that one in four girls and one in twenty boys will be victims of sexual abuse before the age of eighteen.[2] Most of us have heard similar statistics so often that we have become desensitized to the hurt and horror they represent.

In well over 90 percent of reported cases, the abuser is someone acquainted with the child.[3] This means that warning children about "stranger danger" is not enough precaution; family members and trusted authority figures pose the greatest threats to a child's sexual safety.

I know the truth of that statement. I was molested by the stereotypical dirty old man I didn't know when I was seven. But the most painful sexual abuse episode came at the hands of my step-uncle the summer of my eleventh birthday. I totally blocked all memory of that terrifying experience for over three decades.

Like many adults who are victims of incest, I did not identify myself as an incest survivor because I narrowly defined incest as sexual intercourse only. Voices in Action, an organization dedicated to helping incest survivors, defines incest as "a betrayal of trust involving overt or covert sexual actions—direct or indirect, verbal or physical (which may include—but is not limited to—intercourse)—between a child and a trusted adult and/or authority figure."

The trusted person might be a parent, grandparent, stepparent, babysitter, older sibling, mom's boyfriend, teacher, pastor, family doctor, coach, or scout leader.

Incest is more about the abuser's need for dominance and control than about sex per se. The incest offender is trying to meet emotional intimacy needs with someone he (most perpetrators are male) can control and dominate. By being sexual with someone less powerful (usually a child), the abuser eliminates the possibility of being rejected by a more suitable adult partner or spouse. To create the illusion of being desired, many incest perpetrators force their victims to say "I love you," "I like this," or something similar during or immediately after the abuse.

Like physical abuse, sexual abuse takes many forms. Among them are these:

- Sexual innuendoes, jokes, comments, looking, leering
- Sexual stimulating, fondling, and touching
- Exposing self to or masturbating in front of a child
- Mutual masturbation

- Oral, anal, or vaginal intercourse (*rape* is the more accurate term)
- Penetration with finger or objects
- Stripping and sexual punishments (e.g., enemas, attaching wires to genitals)
- Forcing children to have sex with each other or with animals
- Watching others have sex or be abused sexually
- Sexual "games" or torture (e.g., burning)
- Pornography—taking pictures of a child or forcing a child to watch pornography

You may feel sad, angry, or uneasy as you consider the ways in which children are sexually abused. Certainly, God is angry about all forms of child abuse, and His heart must be broken by the pain and brokenness of incest survivors. It is never wrong to feel what God feels.

Some forms of incest are subtle, hands-off, and therefore even more confusing than overt incest.

Faith remembers that in her strict, religious family, she and her two sisters were called "whores" for wearing pants or shorts. This kind of sexualizing of nonsexual behavior is common in homes where no overt sexual abuse ever takes place. Mixed messages about sexuality abound. Not all are as blatant as this ridiculous but actual statement: "Sex is filthy and disgusting; save it for the one you love and marry!" But all are misleading, confusing, unbiblical, and unhealthy.

> **God is angry about all forms of child abuse.... It is never wrong to feel what God feels.**

Incest survivors often feel like damaged goods. And if they do not remember any childhood abuse, they have no way to make sense of their deep-seated feelings of self-hatred and shame.

You probably won't be surprised to learn that sexual and physical abuse survivors also have problems trusting appropriately. That makes perfect sense, as those crimes against children are fundamentally betrayals of trust.

Parents and other adult authority figures who neglect and abuse children in these and other ways are *trust bandits*. They steal a child's capacity for trust, with profound effects on the child's later relationships with God and others.

Parents Who Lie to Their Children

The neglect and abuse by bandit-parents send loud and clear messages, and these messages overflow with lies.

Some lies are more destructive than others. "Easy to assemble" and "one size fits all" are two relatively benign untruths. These are more malignant lies: "I can do anything I want because I'm your parent" and "You're disrespecting your elders when you object to Grandpa's kisses."

Lies about Normal Needs and Personal Worth

Perpetrator-defined reality is one of the distinguishing characteristics of all abusive systems, including abusive family systems. I have counseled many adults who live downwind from the fallout of perpetrator-defined realities. One of the most common of these abuser-twisted realities takes a child's normal needs for nurturing and physical touch and relabels them as sexual come-ons. Perpetrators choose this devastating deception in a pathetic, but usually successful, attempt to shift responsibility for sexual child abuse to the child.

Young children are easily deceived, and a parent's lies can redefine reality about a child's personal worth and natural needs. Lynn knows all about that.

"As long as I can remember, my dad has called me a slut," whispered Lynn, a committed Christian in her mid-thirties.

Lynn sought counseling to work on depression and low self-esteem issues that rapidly became despair and intense self-hatred issues. After some months, this bright, caring woman began to experience frightening memory fragments flashing through her mind, followed by intense feelings of terror and a sense that, as Lynn expressed it, "something terrible is about to happen."

The puzzle pieces of Lynn's childhood eventually came together, revealing at least seven years of violent incest involving both her father and his father. From the age of five, when her father and grandfather began to rape and sodomize her, Lynn heard herself called a slut.

But here was Lynn's problem. She didn't know what a slut was. All she knew was that because she was one, it was all right for Daddy and Grandpa to do those painful things.

"It was such an awful, hopeless feeling," Lynn told me, tears streaming down her cheeks. "You see, I didn't know what I did that made me a slut. Even worse, I didn't know how not to be a slut so they would stop doing those hurtful things," she sobbed.

Like all of us, Lynn came into the world needing answers to questions like "Who am I?" and "Is the world a safe place?" Tragically, Lynn's lying caregivers taught her that she was a slut, a so-called fact that disqualified her from living in a safe world.

Children like Lynn learn to expect pain as the price for life and for any kind of relationship.

Clearly, parents who abuse or fail to protect their offspring from abuse, as Lynn's mother did, perpetrate a gigantic, hideous hoax that misrepresents nearly every aspect of healthy family life.

Lies about Abuse

Children in severely abusive families learn a lot of crazy-making lies, and some of the most damaging are those used as proof that abuse is not wrong. Here are three common lies used to rationalize abuse.

1. Abuse is normal. Therefore, your distressing emotional response is wrong, and you are bad for having those feelings. Parents use this lie to minimize and normalize their abusive behavior. When a child musters the courage to object to such treatment, it is common for the perpetrator to call her too sensitive. And some incest survivors, when they begin to recall their childhood sexual abuse, are told by family members, "That was just his way of showing affection." "He" might have been Uncle Joe, Grandpa, or Dad. And "his way" may have included masturbating to orgasm in front of the child, fondling the child's genitals, or even oral, anal, or vaginal rape.

> **Words are powerful tools to convey or conceal truth. And hurtful families use words to minimize and discount abuse.**

Words are powerful tools to convey or conceal truth. And hurtful families use words to minimize and discount abuse and to redefine appropriate victim response as "making a federal case of it" or "causing trouble."

2. Abuse is justified. You have a basic flaw or evil in you that elicits the abuse. Children who grow to become healthy adults label this lie as complete and utter garbage. But for children who believe their parents know everything about everything and always tell the truth, the lie becomes a heavy, hurtful heritage.

3. Abuse is necessary. You have to tolerate it because it keeps the family together. Many incest survivors recall their abusers saying, "If you tell anyone about this, it will break up the family." The message? If the family breaks up, it will be your fault. Since keeping the family together is good, being hurt is necessary.

These three lies are the core curriculum in hurting and hurtful families. But underlying all of them is a fourth lie that all abused children learn first.

4. Being a good child means behaving as if this is a perfect family. Abusive families are deeply invested in maintaining the public image of being perfectly happy and problem-free—no matter

54

how much evidence to the contrary has to be ignored. They are what I call *moon families*.

On planet Earth, we see only one side of the moon; its dark side is visible only via space exploration. There are moon families who carefully conceal their dark side from public view. This is extremely confusing to children who cannot make sense of the world when they hear others say how wonderful, even godly, their abusive parents are.

I once read about a professional clown who hired a hit man to kill his estranged wife.[4] Clowns are supposed to be happy, but this clown apparently had no smile other than the one he put on with grease paint.

In much the same way, abusive parents have no smile other than the one they put on when they are seen in public. But what's even worse, they make their children wear the same false smile.

Jesus had some scathing words for religious leaders who made themselves look good to others while ignoring the condition of their hearts. He called them "beautiful mausoleums—full of dead men's bones, and of foulness and corruption" (Matthew 23:27 TLB).

I suspect that Jesus has the same opinion of abusive family leaders in our day.

Lies about Authority

We live in a time when questions abound about whether governmental agencies are encroaching on family life and eroding parental rights to raise children according to personal beliefs. However, even a cursory look at the daily news is enough to convince us that parental rights must be reasonably tempered with concern for child safety.

Yes, there have been abuses of child protection laws and agencies. Nevertheless, someone needs to step in and help children when parents neglect or abuse them. If we believe the lie that parents have the right to raise their children without any outside interference, we risk becoming unwilling participants in harm done to children. Some parents who believe that the right to control their children is inalienable and inviolate lead frighteningly dark lives and families.

Dark Kingdom Families

When liars and thieves reign from parental thrones, families become dark kingdoms. In dark kingdom households, deception and destruction rule, and offspring exist for the sole purpose of meeting the parents' needs.

One counseling client I worked with had survived a childhood of incest, physical torture, and satanic ritualistic abuse. In counseling it was common for her to leap up from a comfortable chair and huddle in a corner behind the wastebasket. At those times, she was reliving the countless dehumanizing childhood experiences when she was told that she was garbage and that she deserved to eat only garbage. As unbelievable as it may sound, many days she was given nothing to eat but garbage and human waste.

How do children survive the soul-deep wounds of such intense moral and spiritual darkness? This heroic woman I counseled coped, in part, by dividing the horrors of her homelife into memory fragments separated by amnesiac barriers. Her capacity to disconnect her mind from her body and her unbearable circumstances saved her life.

Sometimes I encounter dark kingdom refugees at conferences, and occasionally they follow up our brief conversations by reaching out to me later. After hearing me speak at a church in Chicago, Megan wrote me a ten-page letter describing her childhood of repeated abuses, including desertion by her father and incest at the hands of her uncle.

Her father and uncle were liars and thieves. With words and

actions, they told her that she existed only for their convenience. When the responsibilities of fathering became inconvenient, her dad walked out; when her uncle wanted pleasure, he made her precious little-girl body into a sexual gadget. Their lies were hideous. Megan was a beautiful, unique, special creation of God. There will never be another human being exactly like her. By using lies, they stole the safety, security, and stability that adults owe to every child in their care.

Sadly, Megan had concluded that her father's and uncle's treatment of her was a reflection of something wrong with her. In truth, it was a picture of something wrong with them.

Pause to Ponder and Pray

Ponder

- If reading about physical or sexual abuse of children makes you feel too dizzy, lightheaded, nauseous, or confused to finish, consider talking with a helping professional or pastoral counselor.
- If you do not have a helping person in your life, consider finding one—even if it costs money. Remember, you are worth it! I recommend a Christian counselor knowledgeable in abuse survivor issues. If you are a woman and your abuser was male, I urge you to see a female counselor.
- Finally, continue to commit all of this to the Lord, who loves you more than you will ever know.

Pray

> *Lord, help me to be willing to receive whatever wisdom you want me to have about the hidden parts of my life. Teach me to trust you with my past as well as my present and my future. Amen.*

CHAPTER FIVE

HURT BY CHILDHOOD FANTASIES

As young children, all of us lived in a type of fantasyland. Without realizing it, we used magical thinking and fairy-tale logic to make sense of the world. If our families were reasonably healthy, we outgrew this magical thinking as we began to experience the limitations of our actual abilities.

Unfortunately, not all families are reasonably healthy. That's why, for many of us, these lingering childhood fantasies are strangely familiar.

Fantasy #1: Unlimited Power to Control

The fantasy of unlimited power to control events and people is a primitive, powerful, and cherished illusion of all individuals—children and adults.

Young children with limited abilities to interpret the environment come to think of themselves as the center of the universe and believe that they possess the power to cause events and control other people's actions and emotions.

As I think about this, I picture my grandchildren when they were babies. Life through their eyes looked like this:

8:00 a.m. My diaper is wet, and I'm hungry. My cries make Mommy or Daddy appear with a wonderful bottle of milk and a dry diaper.

10:00 a.m. I'm sleepy. My cries cause Mommy to carry me upstairs for a nap.

Noon. I'm hungry again. My cries bring Mommy with a bottle of milk and something mushy that she feeds me with a spoon.

You get the idea. Young children believe that they have the power to cause events and control people's actions.

Furthermore, to explain to themselves why their lives unfold as they do and why people treat them in certain ways, children develop a kind of fairy-tale logic that says good things happen to good people and bad things happen to bad people.

This is well and good for children born into reasonably healthy families led by consistently adequate parents. But it's devastating and destructive for those in troubled homes. And since no families are perfect and no parents can satisfy every child's desire, all children, to some degree or another, believe the second childhood fantasy.

Fantasy #2: Unlimited Ability to Change People and Situations

When kids discover that not everything goes exactly the way they plan and that not everyone does exactly what they want, what do they do? They redo! This is where fantasy number two takes center stage. In its entirety, it says, "If I work hard enough and become good enough, I can make it turn out differently next time."

The "it" we work to make "turn out differently" is some relationship or situation that hurts us. We want to make sure that we don't take another blow in the same wounded place. The "it" that we are dead set on changing might involve all of our family problems or something less sweeping, like a parent's alcohol abuse. We just want things to be different next time. Unfortunately, the variable that is never considered is that every next time involves the will of another human being. Since we have no power to control the will of any other human, this fantasy launches us on a hopeless, lifelong quest for next times.

It's as if we say to ourselves, "If I can just figure out how to be good enough (or smart enough, pretty enough, athletic enough, religious enough, slim enough, wealthy enough, sexual enough, unsexual enough), I can protect myself from being abused, unloved, abandoned."

> **Childhood fantasies do not automatically drop away as we age. Powerful factors reinforce these fantasies, especially for those of us raised in not-so-healthy homes.**

These fantasies are myths, perpetuated by parents, that keep hurtful families stuck in their unhealthy and unbiblical patterns of living.

Unfortunately, childhood fantasies do not automatically drop away as we age. Powerful factors reinforce these fantasies, especially for those of us raised in not-so-healthy homes.

Childhood fantasy reinforcers fall into two categories: those that all children encounter as a natural part of human development and those experienced primarily in hurting and hurtful families.

Universal Reinforcer #1: Our Own *I*-dolatry

Playing God is exhausting. I know because I tried for years and years. You probably will not be surprised to learn that my Holy Spirit imitation was unconvincing. Even as a dedicated Christian, I approached relationships from this perspective: "God loves you, and Sandy has a wonderful plan for your life." Eventually I realized that my perversion of the phrase popularized by Cru—"God loves you and has a wonderful plan for your life"—was a form of *i*-dolatry.

Lust for Omnipotence

It is interesting to ponder the first childhood fantasy in light of the first temptation in Genesis 3. The Tempter promised Eve that she would become "like God" (v. 5) if she ate fruit from the only off-limits tree in God's garden.

I think I am on target in saying that God is identified more by His omnipotence—unlimited power—than by any other attribute.

Perhaps, then, our most primitive and powerful fantasy has its roots in a temptation so old that it's called original sin. If this is true, it is also true that each of us, in turn, reenacts the Genesis scene as we wrestle with the lust for the power to control our world and its inhabitants.

> **The determination to know everything about how to fix everything and everybody springs from the desire to control everything and everybody.**

Lust for Omniscience

If omnipotence is the most distinct attribute of God, a close second is omniscience—unlimited knowledge about all events and all people for all time. Perhaps you've heard statements such as these to describe God: "God knows the end from the beginning" or "God sees around corners." These are human attempts to describe omniscience.

The lust for omniscience is based on the misbelief that we can figure out how to change anything. That's another way of saying, "I am determined to know everything about how to fix everything and everybody." Of course, the determination to know everything about how to fix everything and everybody springs from the desire to control everything and everybody. Again, the desire to play God is rearing its sin-stained head. None of us have to return to Eden to hear the Tempter's voice.

Universal Reinforcer #2: New Age Spirituality

"Self-empowerment means universal power," claims the title of a self-help article for adults raised in hurting and hurtful families. If we listen closely to this statement, we hear the Eden lie echoing through the corridors of time. The message that human beings have the potential for unlimited power is the Tempter's original lie dressed up in New Age babble. No wonder it is so popular—it panders to our lust for God's omnipotence and omniscience. Humans have a sin-bent longing to be crowned ruler of the universe—or at least of our own universe.

Variations on the New Age theme of unlimited human potential are heard everywhere by everyone to some degree. But I believe there are two other reinforcers of childhood fantasies that are heard primarily (though not exclusively) within the domain of dysfunctional households.

Dysfunctional Reinforcer #1: Parental Stumbling Blocks

"Hang a heavy stone around a person's neck and then drown them in deep water." Sounds like something out of a Mafia handbook, doesn't it? Actually, it is Jesus's recommendation for what should happen to anyone who causes an innocent person to sin (Matthew 18:6–7).

Why would Jesus pronounce such doom on those who cause children to make sinful choices? Perhaps it's because children have limited cognitive development, which prevents them from making good choices. In other words, they do not yet have the ability to filter out untruthful and misleading verbal and behavioral messages sent by hurting and hurtful adults.

If I blamed you for "causing" me to hit you, you would reasonably conclude that I am immature for trying to get you to take responsibility for something I did. You would be right. However, when children are blamed for Mom's rages, Dad's alcoholism, or even their own abuse, they do not yet know that they can disbelieve and disregard such lies. They don't recognize them as the pathetic attempt of an immature, irresponsible adult to shift blame onto an innocent child.

The blaming sounds like this: "You love to make me hit you, don't you?" Or "If you weren't so bad, I wouldn't drink so much."

Children hear and come to believe the lie, "I cause it by who I am." The "it," of course, is anything the adult wants to disown.

Those of us who grew up in families where irresponsible, blame-shifting adults ran the show inevitably gravitate toward another fantasy reinforcer: self-protection.

Dysfunctional Reinforcer #2: Self-Protection

Children in hurtful families need the fantasies spun by childish magical thinking to keep them from drowning in the bottomless horror of helplessness. As painful as it is for children to believe that they are so rotten and worthless that they caused their perfectly nice parents to neglect or abuse them, there is something far worse. It is the terror of acknowledging that their parents choose to hurt them and that they are powerless to stop them.

Stop for a moment to think about how fragile you were as a child, and

> As painful as it is for children to believe that they are so rotten and worthless that they caused their perfectly nice parents to neglect or abuse them, there is something far worse. It is the terror of acknowledging that their parents choose to hurt them.

imagine how terrifying it would have been to feel utterly defenseless.

Children in hurting and hurtful families need the fantasy of omnipotence and omniscience to provide a feeling of protection for themselves. Believing that they caused their mistreatment allows them also to believe that they can control it.

The more chaotic and out of control a child senses his or her family to be, the more determined the child will be to become a skillful controller.

We can work on controlling externals (people and circumstances) or on internals (emotions, thoughts, and memories). Most of us try doing both.

Trying to protect ourselves with fantasies is like trying to stay warm wearing the weavers' invisible clothing in "The Emperor's New Clothes." The new clothes were not real, and neither are our fantasies, but we believe in them because they make us feel more powerful and safe.

Unfortunately, these fantasies go with us into our adult lives. And the deeper our wounds from childhood, the more likely we are to base our adult lives on self-protective fantasies.

In a way, all adult relationships are a type of family reunion. When looking for friends and lovers, we unknowingly scan the environment for people who resemble our earliest and most significant others—parents or other important adults from childhood, perhaps even an incest perpetrator.

Each relationship becomes an opportunity to rewrite the ending of the original interaction and make it happier.

For example, adult incest survivors often wear loose—even baggy—clothing that conceals the contours of their bodies. They still believe that their bodies caused a perfectly nice person to molest them. So, they think that by hiding their shape, they can make interactions with potential perpetrators end differently.

However, these same survivors may also screen out any awareness of sexually unsafe situations, putting themselves unnecessarily at risk to rape and other forms of sexual abuse. That's the problem with self-protective fantasies. They can't keep us safe. Many see painful and baffling similarities in all their adult relationships because they are relating out of unrecognized fantasies.

Fairy tales and fantasies are harmless when they're identified as such. But the tragedy is that they have painful, life-changing effects when adults continue to believe that they are true.

When a Fantasy Becomes a Tragedy

As a Bible teacher, informal people helper, and then counselor and conference speaker, I've heard many heartbreaking, gut-twisting stories of childhood pain. But few of them compare with the one Karen told me.

Karen is an attractive young woman who is a devoted wife and mother and a committed Christian. She is also working hard to correct all the distorted thinking she learned as a child in a very hurting and hurtful family. Karen's dad worked in Middle Eastern oil fields, which took him away from the family for long stretches of time. That was difficult enough to handle, but what made it even worse was that Karen's mother was schizophrenic, so there was no one at home to protect her from a sexual predator. This is how she describes what happened.

> The summer I was five, the elderly man across the street molested me several times in his basement. One time his wife even came down and saw what he was doing. I thought she'd help me and make him stop, but she didn't say or do anything. I didn't understand what was happening, but I knew it was wrong and I really, really wanted it to stop.

I tried to tell my mother so she would make him quit, but I should have known better. She only fell apart. She put me in the bathtub and scrubbed so hard I thought my skin would come off. As she scrubbed, she yelled and screamed, "Bad, dirty little girl. God can't love bad, dirty little girls."

I just knew that what he did made me filthy, and because I was a bad, dirty little girl, my mommy and God couldn't love me. Somehow I had to get rid of him and make myself clean enough and good enough to be loved.

I hate myself for what I did to my body—how I hurt myself. I've always been afraid of God's anger at me for what I did to myself, especially now.

Karen's now included a probable colostomy due to irreparable damage to her body. In a desperate attempt to cleanse her body from the filth of her sexual abuse, Karen had scraped away multiple layers of anal tissue.

Clearly, Karen's life was altered tragically by her childhood fantasy that said, "I can fix it. I can change the outcome by making myself clean enough to earn Mommy's and God's love."

In counseling, Karen eventually was able to see herself as the helpless little girl she was when she was sexually abused. She realized too how logical, from a child's perspective, her choice had been.

I invited Karen to enter, in her imagination, the bathroom where that little girl sat in bloody bathwater after being emotionally abandoned by her mentally disturbed mother. I asked her to do and say what that desolate child needed to hear at that desperate moment. Karen wept as she told her child-self the truth she had needed to hear for so many years: "You didn't cause it, and it wasn't your fault. God has always loved you and always will. God is angry about what the abuser did to your body. He is not angry about what you did to your body because He understands that you did the best you knew to do as a little child. You are a very brave little girl, and I am so sorry you were hurt so badly."

Few of us will have such devastating proof of the power of childhood fantasies. Yet all of us must come to recognize their impact on our hurting and hurtful ways if we want to realize the promise of healing.

Pause to Ponder and Pray

Ponder

Read the following statements and check the ones that describe your views:

- If I were a better person (or better Christian), I could change my spouse, child, friend, or colleague.
- If someone disagrees with me, his or her opinions are usually right.
- I am responsible for the problems in my family (or office, Bible study, etc.).
- When things go wrong, it's usually my fault.
- If I did _____, then _____ (my spouse, child, friend, etc.) would do _____. (E.g., "If I would start sleeping with my boyfriend like he asks me to, then he would not view so much pornography or threaten to date other women.")

All of the above statements reveal the influence of childhood fantasies.

Truth-based perceptions include:

- I do not have the power to change anyone, no matter how much better I get.
- My opinions are as valid as anyone else's.
- I share responsibility for the atmosphere of my family, office, or Bible study.
- When things go wrong, I am sometimes responsible, sometimes partly responsible, and sometimes not responsible.
- Sleeping with my boyfriend (or whatever with whomever) has no bearing on whether or not he leaves me or views pornography. He is responsible for choosing those behaviors.

Pray

> *Lord, help me to trust you enough to let you
> be who you and you alone are—the Event
> Controller and People Changer. Thank you
> for understanding how difficult this is for me
> because of the deeply wounding circumstances
> that you have allowed in my life. Amen.*

CHAPTER SIX

HURT BY CHILDHOOD CHOICES

In great measure, our lives equal the sum of our choices. And our earliest, most basic choice is to stay alive. All subsequent decisions are founded on, structured by, and supportive of that primal, life-affirming choice. Who we become is the result of thousands of choices made over decades of living, the majority of which are in response to three questions every human being answers repeatedly from the moment of birth:

Can I be safe?

Can I be me?

Can I be accepted?

Our earliest responses to these questions form the fountainhead from which flow other spiritual, personal, and relational decisions throughout life. All of us begin making these life-shaping choices as young, easily confused (perhaps even abused) children who lack the cognitive development necessary to accurately interpret the events going on around us.

We shouldn't be surprised that our responses to these three questions depend on the level of safety, security, and stability we sensed in our first universe—our family. Nor is it surprising

69

that many of us have hurt ourselves and others as we've lived out our early childhood choices.

Childhood Choice #1: Can I Be Safe?

The first question involves trust. Each of us made our early choices based on our perceptions and conclusions about whether or not our newborn universes—our families—were safe places. If our homes were reasonably healthy and stable, we concluded that we could depend on our parents and other adults to recognize and meet our needs. We sensed that we could trust them to take care of us and keep us safe.

Children generally think of God as an exaggerated parent. If we had competent, trustworthy parents, we likely concluded that God too could be trusted to know and meet our needs, care for us, and keep us safe.

As we got older, we realized that our trustworthy and loving God never promised to keep us free of the pain or immune from the blows of an unsafe world. So, we had to learn how to balance the truth of God's constant care with the reality of life's unceasing uncertainties and relentless risks.

> When young children sense a lack of safety, they begin restructuring their environment to make it safe—at least safe enough for survival.

In contrast, if we were born into an unstable household, we learned that we could not depend on parents and adults to recognize and meet our needs. We sensed that our surroundings were not safe and that it was up to us to figure out how to keep ourselves safe, since none of the big people could be trusted to take care of us and make us feel safe.

So, if we had parents who were not trustworthy, we probably assumed that our heavenly Parent could not be trusted either. After

70

all, if God is in charge of everything (as most churches teach), then He is responsible for our inadequate and unsafe parents. In effect, this choice says, "Since my parents cannot be trusted to keep me safe, God (if there is one) cannot be trusted either."

When young children sense a lack of safety, they begin restructuring their environment to make it safe—at least safe enough for survival. In so doing, they prolong the normal magical thinking of childhood by keeping themselves at the center of their personal universe. When we believe that we can only trust ourselves for our safety, everything in life centers on us. That's why our response to the second question is so significant.

Childhood Choice #2: Can I Be Me?

The question "Can I be me?" is show-and-tell at its most nitty-gritty. It asks whether it is safe to know ourselves and show ourselves to family members. Worded differently, this question asks, "Is it safe to recognize and express my authentic, human, sometimes messy and unpleasant needs and feelings and all the other elements of my real self—flaws included?"

If it is safe, we usually resolve to know ourselves and show ourselves as honestly as possible.

We transfer this attitude to our relationship with God, believing that He wants us to be honest with Him about our feelings and needs. After all, God created us with certain needs and feelings, so why would He reject us for having them? What's more, He knows us far better than we will ever know ourselves, and He loves us still.

In hurting and hurtful families, however, children learn that it is not safe to put their identities on the line. Their real needs and feelings are bothersome and bad. It isn't safe to show them because parents are absorbed in their own needs and feelings. If children reveal natural, normal neediness and vulnerability, parents withdraw emotionally, attack brutally, or, more likely, respond with a mixture of both. One way or another, parents convey the message, "You aren't allowed to have needs and feelings because mine absorb all of my energy and interests."

Out of this awareness, many children determine that the best way to meet their own needs is to eliminate them. It hurts too much to recognize and reveal needs time after time without having them met.

> **Many children determine that the best way to meet their own needs is to eliminate them. It hurts too much to recognize and reveal needs time after time without having them met.**

Eventually, children give up hope of having their needs met, so they try to stop having them. The problem is that denying needs and deadening feelings does not make them disappear. They merely take on a disguise and show up later as something else—often something surprising and hurtful.

The reasoning behind the choice to conceal needs and emotions is something like this: "Being myself and expressing needs brings emotional (or sometimes even physical) pain. I am a huge disappointment and a colossal burden to the people who are supposed to take care of me. I will hide my thoughts and feelings and struggles or I won't survive."

Needs and feelings are major components of who we are, but the logical conclusion for a child is, "Needs and feelings are bad, and I must be bad for having them. To keep myself safe, I must not show my neediness, my vulnerability, or my imperfection. And the safest way to keep from accidentally *showing* the real me is to avoid *knowing* the real me. So, I will stop tuning in to my longings and emotions. Yeah, that will work. No genuine personal needs. No real feelings or flaws. That's the ticket."

Clearly, as children we lacked the psychological sophistication to reason our way through the maze of perceptions to reach the conclusions spelled out above.

Clearly too, the amount of hurting in our families directly affects how intensely we continue to choose to mask our identities and hide our imperfections. But no matter how heavy our masks become, we keep wearing them. Because the alternative is worse—being seen for who we are and being deemed unacceptable.

Childhood Choice #3: Can I Be Accepted?

People don't just have relationships; they are relational. This reality explains our intense need to be accepted and found eligible for relationships—in a word, loved.

Ideally, parents love their children for no good reason; that is, they love them simply because they are their children. That certainly is the biblical model.

God in His sovereignty chose to set His love on us when there was nothing lovable about us (Romans 5:8). In other words, our love relationship with God was totally one-sided at first. But it doesn't end there.

When we choose to love God, we do so "because he first loved us" (1 John 4:19). People who are loved become people who can love. The same is true in human families. Children who are secure in their parents' love develop loving natures that they express through their own unique personalities.

In the mind of a child from a safe, stable home, self-talk sounds like this: "My parents love me for no particular reason. They accept and love me even when I make lots of mistakes. I love my folks too and really want to please them, even though what I do or don't do doesn't seem to affect how much they love me."

Such children carry this reasoning into the spiritual realm as well, thinking, "God is my heavenly Father, so He too accepts and loves me even though He knows all about me and my mistakes—even more than my parents know. I love God because He loves me, and I want to obey Him because I love Him."

In contrast to this secure and settled sense of being loved—flaws and all—children raised by impaired, shame-bound parents tend to rehearse a very different mental monologue: "Just being me isn't good enough to get approval and love. My parents will accept me only if I work harder to please them, but I never seem to be quite good enough to earn their full acceptance and love. If I keep trying to figure out how to please them, maybe someday I'll earn their seal of approval and love."

> **Children raised by impaired, shame-bound parents tend to rehearse a very different mental monologue: "Just being me isn't good enough to get approval and love."**

These children also carry their reasoning into the spiritual realm, thinking, "God, my heavenly Father, loves me more when I do more religious performing. Since I'm never sure that I please God, I'll just keep working harder at being good so I can earn His love."

The following chart summarizes the contrasting choices made in different types of families.

Primary Choice of All Children: Stay Alive

	Child's Basic Choice in Safe, Secure, Stable Family	Child's Basic Choice in Unsafe, Insecure, Unstable Family
Spiritual Arena of Trust Universal Question: Can I Be Safe?	I will trust my parents to keep me safe now. I will trust myself to keep me safe when I am bigger. I will trust God to keep me safe always.	I will trust only myself, now and always.
Personal Arena of Identity Universal Question: Can I Be Me?	I will know and show who I really am.	I will hide who I really am from myself and from others.

	Child's Basic Choice in Safe, Secure, Stable Family	Child's Basic Choice in Unsafe, Insecure, Unstable Family
Relational Arena of Attachment Universal Question: Can I Be Accepted?	I will accept myself since I am accepted by those who love me.	I will try hard to be good enough to earn acceptance and to be loved.
Summary of Contrasting Child Choices	**Child from Consistently Stable Family**	**Child from Consistently Unstable Family**
	I will trust trustworthy people and God. I can be, know, and develop because I am accepted for myself in real love relationships.	I will trust myself to stay safe by hiding the real me from myself and from others. I'll try to please others so I can be good enough to earn acceptance and love.

Which of these basic choice patterns is more familiar? For me, it was the second.

My Childhood Choices Legacy

I was launched into a performance-based lifestyle by the time I was five. Shortly before my fifth birthday, I began piano lessons and was playing at churches and community gatherings within a few months. Some of my earliest pleasant memories feature my mother's smiling face as she basked in the glow of compliments about her "talented little daughter." I wasn't that good, but Phoenix was a small place then, and there was a shortage of five-year-old pianists.

Like any child, I lapped up all the attention and approval. The man I knew as my father was away fighting World War II. My mom worked all day at the hospital and often spent evenings downtown packing parachutes. The elderly couple we rented a room from took care of me but remained emotionally detached.

I knew my mother loved me because she told me she did, but I felt more secure when I made her feel proud and happy, when I earned her smile. She seemed to be happiest when others complimented her about something I had done.

I know now that my mother was emotionally wounded and insecure because she grew up feeling unloved by her mother and alienated from many of her brothers and sisters. She determined early to earn her place by being useful, so she sewed a lot of her sisters' clothes, worked in the fields as long and as hard as her brothers, and still managed to become the valedictorian of her high school class.

My mother chose performance as a way of keeping herself safe in a family universe that mixed acceptance with alienation and made her feel insecure. She also chose to hide her real needs and feelings. She learned early that expressing them made her feel worse because she would have to feel the added pain of realizing that her needs weren't important to anyone. By choosing to be good enough, smart enough, helpful enough, and whatever else enough, she thought she could earn acceptance.

Without saying a word, my mother taught me how to keep myself safe by hiding the real me while pleasing and performing to earn her acceptance. And I was a fast learner.

Clearly, our life-shaping childhood choices are shaped by our parents' life-shaping childhood choices, which were shaped by the generation before, and so on. Whatever our childhood circumstances, because of normal developmental limitations, we had no option except to receive everything our parents and other adults modeled and told us was "Truth" with a capital *T*.

Childhood Stumbling and Childhood Choices

When Jesus spoke about causing a child to stumble in Matthew 18, He was addressing spiritual issues. However, we can make a broader application. The word translated "stumble" in verse 6 pictures how parents and other adults cause children to trip and fall over obstacles of false teaching placed in the children's paths.[1]

The primary reason children stumble is because they believe that adults know everything and tell the truth about everything. This natural but naive and erroneous assumption gives adults the power to create the universe children live in, distort the thinking that informs their decisions, and cause children to fall into hurtful and harmful patterns of behavior. Let me illustrate.

Since I was born into an English-speaking family, I grew up in an English-speaking universe. Living in an English-speaking universe in America meant that I didn't know other languages existed. My speaking options were English or English. I couldn't wake up one morning and choose to speak Spanish or Chinese. I had no choice but to think and speak my parents' language. Without at least two options, we do not have genuine choice.

When I got older and noticed that some families did not speak English, I might have asked my parents to explain. Normal, healthy parents would have told me about other countries, other cultures, and other languages. But abnormal, unhealthy parents might call me stupid (or crazy) for even thinking about the possibility of speaking another language. Or they might make veiled threats of emotional abandonment with statements like, "No kid of mine is going to go around speaking some foreign language."

If my parents were of the latter type, I would have heard the implication that I was disloyal to even raise the language issue, and if I wanted to remain a part of their family, I had better learn to think and speak their way. Since I had no alternative source of food, shelter, and other necessities, I would have had no choice but to adopt my parents' presentation of reality, including their perspective on acceptable language. To fully appreciate parental power in such circumstances, we must remember that long after children are able to survive physical abandonment, threats of emotional abandonment continue to feel life-threatening.

Without recognizing my self-protective choice, I would have embraced my parents' English-only perspective as the one true, morally upright (perhaps even biblical) worldview. What's more, I would have believed that I chose it freely, when in fact I had no other option except becoming an emotional orphan.

> **Long after children are able to survive physical abandonment, threats of emotional abandonment continue to feel life-threatening.**

I would have subsequently sifted every experience through that perceptual filter. To maintain my loyal child status, and thereby avoid the pain of emotional abandonment, I would have continued to exclude other language choices—even as an adult.

Adult Pain from Childhood Choices

Tragically, many of us continue to live out our early childhood choices year after pain-filled year as if we have no more options now than when we were parent-dependent kids. But we do.

As adults, we have choices today that we did not have as children. Parents and other adults no longer have the power to control our perceptions of reality unless we give it to them. If we do, we forfeit our ability to think and decide for ourselves. We stay childified as we continue to grow old without growing up.

And here's the tricky part about this mess: we usually have no clue that we are making such a decision.

Pause to Ponder and Pray

Ponder

Reread the chart summarizing the basic choices made in early childhood in response to the questions of trust, identity, and attachment. Then answer the following questions:

1. Do I tend to over-trust by assuming that everyone is trustworthy?
2. Do I tend to under-trust by assuming that people who have demonstrated consistent (but imperfect) trustworthiness are untrustworthy?
3. What is my trusting style?
4. On a scale of 1 to 10, how well do I know myself? (1 = clueless; 10 = totally)
5. On a scale of 1 to 10, how well do I accept myself? (1 = not at all; 10= totally)
6. In twenty-five words or less, write a life-choices statement for yourself. Include a phrase addressing trust, identity, and attachment issues like the summary statements in the chart.

Pray

> *Lord, help me to see how I used your awesome gift of choice to protect myself as a child. Please show me the ways that my childhood choices are hurting me and those I love. Thank you for being so patient with me as I fear and falter in this scary process of letting you give me wisdom in the hidden parts of my life. Amen.*

PART 2

OUR HELP AND HOPE

CHAPTER SEVEN
HELP FOR HEALING OUR HURTS

Most of our adult life problems are the result of childhood solutions.

In other words, something happened a long time ago that hurt us. We protected ourselves the only way we knew how. But somewhere along the way to adulthood, our method stopped working.

Childhood solutions are naturally self-protective, and they express childhood perceptions and choices. We see a dramatic example of childhood solutions becoming adult life problems in adults who develop dissociative identity disorder (multiple personality disorder).

As children, people with dissociative identity disorder disconnected from unbearable trauma by creating mental companions to help them bear it. Not surprisingly, the sanity-saving behavior of childhood becomes a confusion-causing problem in adult life.

Since amnesia usually separates these mental companions, one personality may know nothing about the others. Multiples learn to fake knowing someone or something that is remembered only by a part of them that isn't in charge at the moment.

Obviously, this requires intelligence and practice. Obviously, too, multiples experience great confusion and expend enormous energy concealing their sense of inner fragmentation. It's easy to see how a multiple's childhood solution to overwhelming trauma becomes his or her major adult life problem.

Since most of us do not have dissociative identity disorder, we may miss the more subtle manifestations of this principle in our lives. I did for a long time.

As a youngster, I decided to solve the problem of my mother's overworked, under-loved, single-parent sadness by performing as well as possible and as often as possible to earn compliments for her and to earn acceptance and a greater sense of personal safety for me. That solution worked so well for me that I used it over and over.

By the time I was an adult, I had become a world-class performer and people pleaser. I directed most of my energy to polishing my performances rather than developing my character, which, as you can imagine, caused a lot of problems for me and for those dearest to me.

Whether we are multiples, perfectionistic performers and pleasers, or hurting and hurtful in some other way, we have one thing in common. A long time ago we had a scary and painful problem; we chose the best solution we could at the time, but it isn't working anymore. Our solutions have become our problems. Clearly, something's got to change.

Some Preliminaries to Change

Where do we typically focus when we want to change? Our adult lifestyles and relationships, right? That's only natural. But our adult lives, with their hurting and hurtful ways, are the composites of earlier repeated choices. Here's what I mean: "What we live with, we learn, and what we learn, we practice. What we practice, we become, and what we become has consequences."[1]

Most people seek counseling of one kind or another—whether formal and expensive with a therapist in an office or informal and free with a friend over coffee—because of the painful consequences of their prevailing life patterns.

That's what I did. And I looked for someone or something that would help me get different consequences from the same old choices.

Like many people, I ran around grumbling about the sickly fruit that my life was producing without bothering to look at the seeds or the soil. I expected to keep sowing the same seed in the same soil and yet reap a different crop.

Put that way, my expectation not only sounds unrealistic—it sounds insane. If we want genuine change in the fruit of our lives, we must first clear out the weeds of deception, loosen the soil with honesty, and then sow seeds of truth.

In other words, if we want new consequences, we must make new choices. And if we do, our lives will change.

Wilson's Theory of Change

For years at conferences and in seminary classes I discussed my theory as to what produces change. Granted, it's not very complex or elegant, but it covers the basics. Wilson's Theory of Change says, "Making and consistently practicing new choices produces change."

If you like equations, it looks like this:

New Choices + Consistent Practice = Change

Here, of course, I'm discussing change from a human perspective. We must remember that our change efforts have eternal significance only when they are empowered by the Holy Spirit of God. To do our part well in the change process, we need to look more closely at our choices.

Owning Our Choices

Have you ever stopped to consider that we cannot change what we did not choose? We confront that reality when we work in vain to change other people's choices.

> Recognizing and reclaiming our choices is a prerequisite to changing those choices. And changing our choices is at the heart of changing our lives and relationships.

Perhaps even more germane to our immediate discussion is this: *We won't know we can change what we don't know we have chosen.* This means that recognizing and reclaiming our choices is a prerequisite to changing those choices. And changing our choices is at the heart of changing our lives and relationships.

The process of reviewing our childhood perceptions and choices fits the assignment given by the apostle Paul to a group of struggling (dare I say hurting and hurtful) Christians in the first century. "Put away childish things" he told them (1 Corinthians 13:11 NKJV). To become mature requires that we let go of our childish ways.

How would the apostle Paul, the Corinthian Christians, you, I, or anyone else know what to "put away" without reviewing and reevaluating our childhood perceptions and choices from a more mature—hopefully wiser—perspective? After all, when we were children, everything we believed may have *been* childish, but nothing we believed would have *seemed* childish. It seemed normal. And our easy acceptance of family realities as ultimate reality makes putting away childish things quite a challenge.

In *Putting Away Childish Things*, pastor and counselor David Seamands writes, "Childish things don't simply fall away by themselves as dead leaves fall from a tree. We have to put them away, *katargeo* them, and be 'finished with childish things.'"[2]

The Greek verb *katargeo* means "to abolish, wipe out, set aside something."[3] Those phrases picture a powerful, purposeful, energetic endeavor, not an automatic or casual occurrence. We may outgrow acne, but childhood misperceptions must be purposefully set aside and replaced with accurate understanding.

Take this quiz to find out if you're ready to proceed to the heart of change.

1. Does it seem reasonable that change requires making new choices and practicing them consistently (though imperfectly)?
2. Can you see that this process requires commitment and hard work?
3. Are you convinced that commitment to change requires that you review and reevaluate your early choices to determine which are based on truth and which on falsehood?

If you answered all three questions affirmatively, you're ready to face the challenges of change.

A Plan for Change

The following chart shows the elements and process involved in change.

Cannot Change	Can Change			
1A	2	3	4	5
• Parents' sin natures • Parents' genetic predisposition and natural endowments • Parents' belief systems • Parents' personal issues • Parents' attitudes and actions toward me • Family atmosphere (e.g., how stable)	My perceptions about #1 i.e., the messages I received	My conclusions about #1 and #2 i.e., what should be done to solve the family problem	My choices about #1, #2, and #3 i.e., my part of the solution to the problem	My life patterns and problems i.e., relationships with self, God, and others
1B				
• My sin nature • My genetic nature				
Part of Childhood				
	Part of Adulthood			

Let's look at each element, noticing specifically which can be changed and which cannot.

Elements We Cannot Change

The column on the left is different from the others for two reasons. First, it is the only column divided into two sections. Second, it is the only one containing elements that are outside our ability to choose and therefore outside our ability to change.

These fixed elements include:

- Our parents' sin natures
- Our parents' genetic predispositions and natural endowments (e.g., susceptibilities to alcoholism or schizophrenia)
- Our parents' personal issues (e.g., routine responsibilities and life-dominating problems)
- Our parents' attitudes and actions toward us
- Family atmosphere (its safety and stability)
- Our own sin natures
- Our own genetic predispositions and natural endowments

Despite my repeated emphasis on new choices for lasting changes, remember that some components of our lives are unchangeable. No matter how much we'd like to be taller or shorter, we cannot change our height. And as much as we long to have had two adoring parents and a stable birth family, some of us never did and never will.

Nevertheless, compared to the unchangeables, many more elements in life are open to new choices and changes.

> Some components of our lives are unchangeable.... As much as we long to have had two adoring parents and a stable birth family, some of us never did and never will.

Elements We Can Change

Look again at the change-plan chart and notice that three of the elements exist as parts of both childhood and adult life: early perceptions, conclusions, and choices. A fourth element, represented by column five, belongs exclusively to adult life while also being the sum, in large part, of everything depicted in columns one through four.

As you can see, we must be willing to identify and reevaluate our childhood fantasies (perceptions and conclusions) and our childhood choices so that we will better understand our adult way of life. That reviewing process gives us a more complete context in which to make new choices.

For example, if our parents were too distracted by their own unacknowledged life-dominating problems and pain to be appropriately nurturing, we learned to discount and deny our natural needs and normal feelings. In effect, our folks sent this message: "I can't take it when you have needs or make requests and demands." In response, our life-affirming, self-protective choice most likely was this: "I won't ever have any need for nurturing. That way my folks won't be upset and overwhelmed. And that way I won't have to face how really unavailable and inadequate they are."

Painfully and paradoxically, the child then begins to take care of the parents (by appearing to have no needs) so that the parents can appear to be taking care of the child.

Here's a summary of this example, using the terms of the change-plan chart.

Parents' Issues and Family Atmosphere	Child's Perceptions	Child's Conclusions
Significantly impaired parents and unsafe, insecure family atmosphere	I will not stay alive without my parents' care, but my parents get upset and are not there for me when I need care.	I will have to protect and take care of my parents (i.e., fix them), so they will be able to protect and take care of me.

Keeping in mind that children have developmentally limited reasoning abilities, what might children in such situations choose to do to keep themselves alive? Here are some possibilities:

- "I will have no needs." (Reasoning: My needs are bad because my needs overwhelm my parents, and then they are even less able to care for me and keep me safe.)

- "I will have no feelings." (Reasoning: Feelings are dangerous because my parents can't tolerate my feelings without getting overwhelmed.)
- "I will try hard to require no care from my parents and to be good enough to make my parents want to care for me and keep me safe." (Reasoning: When I make my needs known, my parents aren't able to care for me, so I get my needs met by not having any needs of my own and by trying to meet theirs.)

Probable Adult Life Patterns

"If we do not change our direction, we are likely to end up where we are headed," says Philip Kotler.[4] With that truth in view, consider this question: What might our adult relational patterns be if we didn't change our direction—that is, if we continued to live and relate based on childhood perceptions, conclusions, and choices like those in the example above? These are some probable outcomes of ending up where we were headed:

- *In our relationship with God*: We would tend to believe that we earn our right standing with God by doing as much as possible for Him while asking as little as possible from Him.
- *In our relationships with others*: We would likely maximize the caretaking skills we honed by parenting impaired and childified parents. Relatively healthy, well-functioning people wouldn't interest us much because, as we might be overheard saying, "they don't really need me." And we would need to be needed to feel comfortable in relationships.

- *In our relationship with ourselves*: Naturally when we're devoting so much time and energy to taking care of others, there wouldn't be enough left over to take appropriate care of ourselves. Besides, because of the home we grew up in, we learned that we were a remarkable, mutant strain of humans who were born without personal needs.

If we continued living out these probable adult life consequences of the childhood choices described in our illustration, we would eventually burn out or break down from physical, emotional, and spiritual exhaustion.

At least, let's hope so. Because we rarely seek change until the alternative is even worse.

The Change Plan in Action: Karen

Do you remember Karen from chapter 5, who ripped out her own flesh in her heartbreaking quest to be good and clean enough to get Mommy and God to love her? Karen did not begin to heal emotionally and spiritually until she revisited and reviewed her desperate childhood choices. Karen raged and wept as she confronted the truth about the emotionally impoverished, chaotic, and dangerous homelife created by her parents' physical and emotional abandonment.

Only then could she begin to accept God's love and believe He was not angry because of what she did to her body. Only then could she start to genuinely forgive her parents, because her previous attempts to excuse and justify their actions evaporated in the noonday light of truth. Only then could she stop hating and start forgiving the scared little girl who tore herself apart to make herself lovable. And only then—at long last—could that desperate little girl find peace.

In counseling, Karen worked at consistently practicing new

choices about how to think about and relate to herself and others. She learned to set appropriate boundaries and respect her own needs as she worked hard, wept often, and went on working. Today, Karen would tell you that the freeing, healing truth she's gained is worth the high price of change.

The Price of Change

Hidden hurts. Suffocating secrets. Like weeds, they grow relentlessly through the cracks in our souls, threatening to overrun our lives. Why would we hesitate for a millisecond to acknowledge and uncover them, no matter the cost? Yet many of us fear the light of truth that reveals them.

Indeed, truth brings suffering as well as freedom—increased hurting before increasing health.

> **Change is an excruciating blend of losses as well as gains.**

We must enter the change process with open eyes. When we do, we'll see that the necessary truth requires tears, time, and even some terror. Tears? Of course, because change is an excruciating blend of losses as well as gains. Time? Indeed, since quick fixes work only in fantasyland. And some terror? You bet. Letting go of old ways before we firmly grasp the new is terrifying. And woven throughout the tears, time, and terror, we see truth, truth again, and more truth.

Tears about Family Losses as a Price of Change

We can't put our pasts behind us when we've never put them before us. Yet many of us stall on the starting line of change because we fear what we'd lose if we did. We must count the cost of change with ruthless realism. Nowhere is this truer than when it comes to losing the approval and affection of family members.

I once counseled a charming woman who grew up in a

subtly but profoundly unhealthy home. Her family's motto was "Family first." Loosely translated from the original Greek (and knowing what I do about her family), this meant, "Ignore and don't talk about who or what is hurtful in this family." An alternative translation might read, "Don't rock the boat with truth, even if it's the *Titanic*!"

We will never begin the move from hurting to healing until we answer the question, "Whose rules rule?" Because the person who makes the rules we live by is the person who is God to us.

If, in an attempt to gain our parents' seal of approval, we continue to live by the rules of hurting, hurtful parents, we will continue our hurting, hurtful ways. But if we choose to know God and put Him on the throne of our lives, we will begin to live by His rules. And as we've already seen, God takes truth very seriously.

Repeatedly choosing to seek and walk in truth is new, strange, even weird to many people raised in hurtful families who were taught that the loving thing is to distort and deny the truth about their family's hurtful ways.

Calling a thing by its correct name is the beginning of change. Some of us need to begin calling "family loyalty" *lying* if that is its correct name. Be aware, however, that embarking on a truth-based approach to life may make us feel as alien in our families as salmon in the Sahara.

We must face the pain inherent in becoming truth tellers in truth-fearing families. We are foolish to expect reality-phobic family members to jump up, click their heels together, and exclaim, "Oh goody! We've all been wondering when someone would get healthy enough to start changing so that we'd be confronted with our personal and family dysfunction and be dragged kicking and screaming into greater wholeness." It just doesn't work that way.

In unhealthy systems, whether they're families or companies, the person who sees and speaks the problem *becomes* the problem. And instead of working to resolve the problem, such systems focus on removing the problem perceiver. And that painful experience usually brings appropriate grieving and tears.

Truth about Blaming as a Price of Change

I've made much of the fact that children do not have the same choices adults have because of their developmentally limited cognitive abilities. I've described at length how as children we all were caused to stumble into distorted patterns of thinking and choosing, to one degree or another. I believe all of this is true. But now that we are adults, this is not all that is true. Some of us must face the truth that we have gotten bogged down in blaming our parents or other powerful people from childhood.

I never cease to marvel at our tendencies to take a reasonably balanced truth and twist it to serve our self-protective and sin-polluted purposes. Sometimes I do this, and so do some people I've met in counseling or at conferences who say, "Sandy thinks that parents are to blame for all our problems." This always astounds me since I've preached personal responsibility for change in all my books, talks, and counseling relationships.

Sincerely struggling changers usually detour only temporarily onto a parent-blaming track. Sadly, a few folks homestead there. They find support in books, usually written by therapists, who tell them things like "forgiving parents is for wimps." That approach may sell books or attract counseling clients, but it is not genuinely helpful. And clearly, it is not biblical.

Ezekiel 18:20 says that each of us "dies"—that is, experiences the consequences—for our own sins. Not parents dying for children's sins, nor children for parents' sins, but all for their own sins. Even more pertinent to our discussion of parents causing their children to stumble, verse 30 tells us to turn away from all our sins so that they don't "become a stumbling block" to us (NASB). Clearly, there is a transfer of primary responsibility in the stumbling-block department from our parents to us when we become adults. Said differently, we must each take responsibility for our own choices as adults.

One of our most important choices will be to invest the time necessary to underwrite the cost of genuine change.

Time as a Price of Change

So many of us hurting Christians sincerely search for what I call anointed amnesia. We think (and may have been taught) that all memories of unpleasant facts and all manifestations of unpleasant feelings are instantly, totally erased at the moment of salvation. Let's face it, we want an evangelical zap! And if we don't get that, the next best thing is for God to meet our demand for a magical makeover of our unhealthy patterns.

Process is such a detestable concept for many of us raised in unhealthy, all-or-nothing families that the very word is virtually obscene. In fact, I sometime joke about *process* being the p-word. Schooled in dichotomous black-or-white concepts, we learned that on a scale of one to ten, there are only two, not ten, possibilities. One or ten. Period.

> We risk sabotaging our change adventures when we forget to take a process perspective.

Consequently, we usually think in terms of extreme polarities: wrong or right, bad or good. Or more pertinent to our ongoing focus, wounded or well, hurt or healed.

We risk sabotaging our change adventures when we forget to take a process perspective. Said differently, change takes not only tears but time. More accurately, a lifetime. Maybe you know people who have signed up for a thirty-day miracle makeover. Or perhaps you know others who commit to a slightly more realistic six-month recovery program.

Scripture presents the most helpful and realistic plan. It's called mind renewal, and it spans a lifetime (Romans 12:2).

After all, Jesus portrayed Himself as the Great Physician, not the Great Magician.

Consider that the Israelites spent a full generation conquering their enemies after God took them into the promised land. Don't you think God was every bit as much in that generation-long conquering process as He was in bringing them into the land? And what about Moses's forty long years of learning humility, patience, and leadership in the wilderness of Midian?

Even the mighty apostle Paul processed privately for years before God gave him a public platform (Galatians 1:17–2:1). And based on Paul's candid admission of ongoing personal and spiritual struggles, his process was cast clearly in the lifelong mind-renewal mold. No wonder God used him to write about the need for us to keep on being transformed by the continual renewal of our minds (that's a literal rendering of the Greek verb tenses in Romans 12:2).

Perhaps part of our resistance to this change-as-the-journey mindset (rather than a change-as-the-destination mindset) relates to the unappealing prospect of ongoing emotional upheaval.

Terror (Almost) as a Price of Change

I chuckled as I typed the heading to this section because I am imagining two possible responses. Some of you may be thinking, "Terror? There's no terror in changing," while others are saying, "Almost? There's no 'almost' to the terror of changing." Typically, the first response characterizes change rookies, while the second belongs to battle-scarred change veterans.

Change is very scary. If you haven't discovered that, you probably haven't been changing very much. I often use a circus analogy to picture the almost-terror level of fear I hear counseling clients describe in their change struggles. Invariably, their eyes ignite with recognition.

Have you ever watched a trapeze act high above a circus floor? If so, you've seen a performer standing on a tiny platform or hanging from a trapeze bar as someone across the way swings a bar toward him or her. Now put yourself in the place of that performer. You see the trapeze bar coming; you reach out for it. But then, to your horror, you realize that you can't grasp it without letting go of what you're already gripping. And you don't have time to look and see if there's a safety net below!

We spend much of our journey of changing, recovering, mending, and healing in that midair split second of terror between relinquishing the wounding, binding, familiar places and firmly grasping the healing, freeing unfamiliar. And at the beginning of our journey, we probably hang there most of the time. (Sorry, but I'm committed to telling the truth!) That breath-snatching midair stretch of trembly transition is a place of messing up and muddling through where endings alone beckon beginnings. Only losses guarantee gains. This is the place where much of what we've called truth, now unmasked, becomes betrayal. What we thought of as solid rock dissolves to quicksand under our feet.

When we've grown up in families where chaos spelled impending pain and disaster, or at the very least increased emotional neglect, we're allergic to anything that feels off-balance, unstructured, uncertain—in a word, chaotic. We probably won't even like spontaneous. With personal histories like that, no wonder the perfectly normal confusion and chaos of changing feels not just distressing but dangerous, destructive, and, yes, terrifying.

I'm not painting a very soothing scene, I'll admit. Believe me, though, all the tears and years of time and even the terror of transition are worth the joy of changing. But because making and consistently practicing new, more truthful choices is so difficult, we all need more than just a plan. We need power.

A Power Source for Change

We are not truth-seeking, truth-loving creatures by nature—at least not those of us living on this side of Eden. Deceit is the natural current of our lives. So we desperately need a power source—maybe even a motivation source—outside of our natural selves to propel and guide us as we swim upstream by choosing to change by consistently choosing truth.

Have you heard about the farmer who bought a chain saw that was guaranteed to cut five big trees an hour? The day after his purchase, he returned it to the store with obvious frustration. "Five trees an hour? It barely cut five trees the whole day," the angry farmer exclaimed. Puzzled, the store owner took the saw outside, jerked its pull cord, and started the powerful engine. The saw's deafening roar startled the farmer so badly that he stumbled and fell trying to escape. Regaining his balance, he gasped, "What's that noise?"

Cutting trees with a silent chain saw is no more foolish than trying to do recovery or get well in our own strength alone. One of my favorite Scriptures, Zechariah 4:6, captures this truth: "'Not by might nor by power, but by my Spirit,' says the LORD Almighty." We need to understand and commit to change. We need a plan to guide the process. But without the power of God's Spirit energizing our understanding, commitment, and process, we will go through the motions of change without anything significant happening.

Hurt people need deep healing. Mere superficial healing won't do the job. Human helpers can supply a lot of the latter; only God can supply the former. That's because our hurting is rooted in a far deeper issue than childhood experiences.

The Bible describes this in one three-letter word: sin. Sin is not a popular word these days. Nevertheless, Scripture indicates repeatedly that all human beings are sin-stained—more accurately, "dead" spiritually because of our sins (Ephesians

2:1). Jesus Christ had no sin of His own, yet He chose to die for our sins so that we could experience the eternal quality of life that exists only in personal relationship with Him.

We must let Jesus pilot our lives before we can ask Him to power our changing. He won't barge in and take over, but He enters hearts when invited. Of course, we have to own our responsibilities in the injury-recovery, healing-from-hurts changing process. But, just as there is an unseen, inner energy at work in physical healing and change, God's unseen Spirit energizes our emotional and spiritual changing processes when we let Him. As we do our part, God does His inside job to create change of eternal significance.

Pause to Ponder and Pray

Ponder

Great, gaping wounds need a Great Physician. It's too late for that, you say? You feel dead? Then you need a proven death defeater! I am delighted to introduce you to the one and only death-defying healer and greatest life changer of all time: Jesus of Nazareth. (Check out His track record in the first four books of the New Testament.)

The most eternally significant, life-changing choice you will ever make is asking Jesus Christ to supervise your life and your process of healing and changing.

If you haven't done that already, you can do it right now by praying something like the following. Remember, God cares more about your desire to know Him personally than the specific words you say.

Pray

> Dear Jesus, I want to know you personally
> as my Savior, my Friend, and the Lord of

my life. Thank you for promising that I can if I ask. Please come into my life and forgive my sins. Thank you for paying the sin debt I could never pay. Thank you for your gift of love. Please direct and empower my changing process. You know how scary it is for me, so thanks for being my safety net too. Amen.

CHAPTER EIGHT

HELP FOR HEALING SELF-INFLICTED WOUNDS

John made a hit with his support group when he adapted the title of a classic country song to summarize his distress. "Achy breaky heart?" he said. "Man, that's nothin'. I've got an achy breaky life!"

I pictured John as a newborn rodeo contestant plopped atop a wild animal.

Sometimes life feels like that. Without warning and without training, we're dropped into situations that seem to have only one possible outcome: disaster. Achy breaky, here I come.

As if the bumps and bruises inflicted on us by difficult people and troublesome situations are not bad enough, some of us also wound ourselves. Self-inflicted wounds often start when we try to treat our wounds and protect ourselves from further hurt.

Self-Inflicted Self-Concept Wounds

"I'm worth it!" the actor declares directly into the camera while tossing her blonde hair over her shoulder. She might be faking it, but she looks as if she means it.

How about you? Are you worth it? Are you worth knowing, worth respecting, worth loving? What sort of relationship do you have with yourself? Yes, that's right, relationship with yourself. Do you treat yourself like a friend or an enemy? Are you more actively involved in growing, stretching, and healing or in self-inflicted revictimization? Many of us do not think we are worth it—whatever it might be. We feel as if we're nothing or less than nothing. And we treat ourselves accordingly by regularly and relentlessly rewounding ourselves with shame.

Self-Inflicted Shame Wounds

In chapter 1, I described binding shame (as differentiated from biblical shame) as the soul-deep sense of being disgustingly different and worth less than others. This sense of shame grows from a two-pronged lie:

Humans can be perfect.
Humans must be perfect to qualify for life and love, for existence and relationships.

Children learn binding shame if their earliest relationships are characterized by unrealistic expectations, neglect, or abuse. After all, if we hear "You ought to be ashamed" often enough and long enough, we believe it.

Shaming messages are recorded in our brains, which replay the shaming sounds and scenes every time our imperfections and limitations show up in our problems, mistakes, or failures.

Binding shame hinders the changing and healing process because we won't seek change if we can't admit to having problems. Wilson's Law of Radical Recovery says it this way: "We have to see before we'll be free." If we refuse to conduct an honest investigation of the problem-laden harvest of our lives, none of us will face the fears, release the tears, or spend the years necessary to get at the root issues. And how can we do such an investigation when we are supposed to be perfect, problem-free people?

Shame says, "I don't have any wounds—self-inflicted or

otherwise—and I certainly don't need to change. Everything in my life is perfect, but thanks for asking." If there's a remnant of such sentiment lurking in a corner of your mind, you need to know the high price tag attached to it.

Researchers have found that people who ignore their negative feelings are making themselves increasingly and needlessly vulnerable to illness. "Suppressing your emotions, whether it's anger, sadness, grief or frustration, can lead to physical stress on your body," clinical psychologist Victoria Tarratt says. From short-term mental and physical issues, to trouble with anxiety, aggression, and depression, to increased risk for diabetes, heart disease, and even cancer, avoiding the problems in our lives is dangerous.[1]

This research affirms the truth of Scripture, namely that we are foolish when we traffic in deception, especially self-deception. (Proverbs 14:8 is one of many verses addressing this.) We wound ourselves when we let shame slam the door on honesty about hidden psychological distress. We make ourselves sick when we shame ourselves into silence.

> **We can't get help for problems we can't admit we have.**

We can't get help for problems we can't admit we have. Instead, exhausted, discouraged, shame-bound people practice what Jeff VanVonderen calls the three steps of shame: "trying, trying harder, and trying my hardest."[2] But this locks the slammed door behind us, making us prisoners of energy-sapping, life-crushing patterns of perfectionism, since even when we try our hardest, the results rarely satisfy us because they're not good enough.

Self-Inflicted Wounds from Perfectionism

"Not good enough." For some of us, those three words define our lives. Anyone who feels this way is struggling with shame. Along with guilt, shame greases the skids for life-crushing perfectionism. And perfectionism is profoundly wounding.

As a recovering perfectionist, I know how difficult it is to risk being honest about weakness and failure. I relapse regularly. And then I berate myself for not being perfectly recovered from my perfectionism! Why do reasonably intelligent and sane adults think and live like this?

Again, early experiences and choices provide a context for understanding and changing.

Who I am is all I have of me. If who I am—just me, the real me—proves inadequate to secure a safe place in the world and a nurturing level of acceptance and affection, I am disarmed. Since I have no other resources in my *being* with which to fight for approval, I switch from *being* to *doing*. I shift to a performance mode in every relationship—with myself, God, others—and so lose permission to be who I am. Of course, performance-based living becomes painful and frantic since the more I do and the better I do it, the more and better I feel I need to do.

When we live a performance-based life, we give other people the power to determine our feelings of worth and safety. We become approval addicts who do nearly anything for a fix. We jump through behavioral hoops and twist ourselves into emotional pretzels to earn the approval of important people in our lives. And all that hoop jumping and pretzel twisting wounds us deeply.

Some of us learn early in life that we earn approval by being helpful, so we become "helpaholics." We develop a keen radar for folks who need help. But in our helping frenzies, we may neglect our spouses and children, even our own health. Some of us are practically dying to help others. "But, hey, that's what I'm here for, right?" we say. "Besides, they have so many needs and I have none."

Self-Inflicted Wounds from Denying Authentic Needs

As mentioned earlier, many of us decided in childhood that the best way to meet our needs was to eliminate them. The problem is that denying needs doesn't make them disappear.

Ignoring natural human needs is like holding our breath

underwater. We ignore our need for oxygen as long as possible and then feel proud for being able to get along without air. In effect, making ourselves feel bad makes us feel good. We secretly glory in the fact that less hearty humans give up after watching us work longer hours, sleep fewer hours, and eat faster as we rush to our next meeting or people-helping commitment. Surviving a killer schedule bolsters our shame-battered self-concepts.

Remember, shame elicits a kind of existence guilt that whispers, "You have to earn the right to take up space on this planet." So the more shame-bound we are, the more we need to push ourselves to multiply our daily allotment of minutes and maximize our productivity and helpfulness.

If we work, rush, push, help, and keep trying harder, maybe we'll be almost barely good enough to earn the approval of our boss, friend, pastor, or God. And if we push a little harder, we may even earn our parents' approval someday, if our bodies hold up that long.

Scripture declares that we are God's temple and that His Spirit lives in us (1 Corinthians 6:19). And in Psalm 139:14, we read,

> I praise you because I am fearfully and
> wonderfully made;
> your works are wonderful,
> I know that full well.

Indeed, God has made our wonderful bodies, but a lot of us don't yet "know that full well." Consider the evidence.

Many of us wage war on our bodies. Our weapons are sleep deprivation, zero or abusive exercise, chronic dieting, sleeping pills, fasting, overeating, bingeing and purging, and relaxation deprivation, among others. We engage in this temple demolition project for many reasons, including mindless emulation of the self-wounding, body-bashing lifestyles our parents modeled.

Abusers often blame their victims' bodies for causing the

abuse, so some victims hate their bodies for betraying them by attracting the abuser. Others despise their bodies for experiencing orgasm during abuse. The latter is one of the most difficult and humiliating realities that sexual abuse survivors face. They have a hard time sorting through their confusion when a perpetrator uses their sexual response against them with statements like, "See, you really wanted me to do this because it makes you feel good."

One incest survivor felt proud for learning to make herself numb to sexual responsiveness during childhood abuse. That was her way of controlling one small aspect of her out-of-control existence. She and her husband are experiencing the sad reality of how a childhood solution can become an adult life problem. Their situation illustrates how we hurt ourselves and eventually others if, as young children, we had to figure out ways to protect ourselves. Child-size solutions never fit adult-size problems.

An accumulating body of research demonstrates that our bodies and emotions are inextricably bound together in a miraculous merger, which of course we know has been designed by God. This means that we wound our bodies when we wound our emotions.

Self-Inflicted Wounds from Denying Emotions

Some of us practice the "take everything without feeling anything" skill as if it were an Olympic sport.

"'Big boys don't cry.' That's what I remember being told," Carl said as he described his frozen feelings. Carl joined a Christ-centered support group because his marriage and personal life were in trouble. As the group discussed acceptable and unacceptable emotions in their childhood families, Carl began to see some of the roots of his emotional paralysis.

"Big boys aren't ever afraid either," Adam said.

"And big boys don't admit they have problems by joining support groups," I added.

Carl and Adam were the only two men in the nine-person group. This is typical.

But women have their own variation on the unacceptable-emotions theme. For them, anger and confidence are the emotions that are off-limits.

Wilson's Law of Emotions applies here. It says, "Feelings are a fact, and feelings have a history." This means that both men and women feel sadness, fear, and anger—what I call the threatening three—plus a host of other emotions. However, both boys and girls learn early the gender-acceptable emotions of their families, and they begin to filter out all other feelings. Remember, in unhealthy families, *unacceptable* is a code word for "dangerous," because when we do the unacceptable in such families, the result is emotional and even physical pain. Unacceptable feelings are so dangerous, in fact, that they must be denied and disowned—the sooner the better.

> **Feelings are a fact, and feelings have a history.**

Children learn to dispose of unacceptable emotions by dumping them into an "emotion recycling bin," where they are processed and later released as a gender-acceptable feelings. The following diagram depicts this process.

A Comparison of Male and Female Emotion Recycling

Male Emotion Recycling System	Female Emotion Recycling System
Sadness, fear, and all other soft emotions	Anger, confidence, and all other firm emotions
Awareness Threshold	
Anger Bin (i.e., "frustration")	Depression Bin (i.e., "concern")

Most committed Christians believe it is unspiritual to be angry or depressed, so for men, their anger is relabeled as frustration, and for women, depression is called concern.

Anger warrants a special word since many people find intense anger and rage too frightening to express. Feelings like rage have a history and a purpose. They tell us that something is hurt and needs tending.

Christians need to be reminded that anger is not a sin (Ephesians 4:26). And it is certainly not a sin to be angry at what angers God. God is very angry about all forms of child abuse. So why shouldn't we be? And why should we be any less angry about it when the child is you or me?

Since feelings are a fact, denying, disowning, recycling, or relabeling them is not the same as destroying them. And research indicates that we wound ourselves when we refuse to recognize and respect pieces of our God-given emotional natures.

We also wound ourselves when we try to deaden our emotions with addictions.

Wounds from Addictions

Addictions serve as emotional anesthetics. They help us self-medicate against the pain of living—especially the pain we think we shouldn't have.

I've heard so many of my counseling clients say, "I don't know what's wrong with me. I shouldn't feel like this." No matter what feelings they're referring to, they have one thing in common: they didn't reckon on the second half of Wilson's Law of Emotions that "feelings have a history."

Feelings don't appear out of nowhere. Even if the history is primarily biochemical, having an accurate context is essential.

Those who grew up in unhealthy families often face a double bind with emotions. Those households typically elicit stronger emotions than do less chaotic homes. At the same time, these hurtful families typically forbid most feelings. Consequently, children lack permission to feel authentic emotions and never learn the skills to express them appropriately.

> In unhealthy families . . . children lack permission to feel authentic emotions and never learn the skills to express them appropriately.

Children raised in emotion-denying homes come into adolescence and adulthood desperate for substances or activities that will deaden disallowed and disowned feelings—the feelings they have been told they shouldn't have but do.

As I've confessed for years, my drug of choice is chocolate. Chocolate is an example of an internal addiction, a substance that we put *into* our bodies. The list of internal addictions is endless. So is the list of external addictions, which includes gambling, working, true-crime podcasts, viewing pornography—any activity, event, or behavior that takes over our lives. What do all of these have in common? They all have the ability to produce a pleasurable mood change. And this is the purpose of all addictions. However, all addictions—whether to booze, bonbons, or bargains—have built-in problems.

First, all addictions have the same annoying side effect: they wear off.

Second, all addictions get greedy. They start demanding bigger and bigger chunks of our thoughts, time, money, energy, integrity, and reputation. Eventually it takes too much of them to give us too little of the positive emotional lift we're seeking.

Third, all addictions ultimately add pain to our lives instead of subtracting it.

The truth behind these three points is this: when we use substances or activities to eliminate pain, we are on a fool's errand of insisting on the impossible. Mark it down: life brings pain, unavoidable pain. And the more we refuse to face our feelings and the unavoidable pain of our unique histories, the more likely we are to keep searching for increasingly powerful mood-altering fixes.

Christians have their own approved addictions. Compulsive shopping and overspending rarely get mentioned. People would gawk if someone staggered drunk down the aisle on a Sunday morning, yet week after week men and women killing themselves with obesity or disordered eating all but stagger down the aisles of churches without notice. Some even stand behind the pulpit. And the sanctified workaholism that masquerades as religious devotion usually earns congratulations rather than compassionate confrontations.

Clearly, what begins as self-defensive protection quickly becomes a self-defeating problem. What is not so clear is how we can change such a pattern.

Applying the Change Plan to Self-Inflicted Wounds

As we start to focus on changing our self-wounding ways, I have two caveats. The first is a reminder; the second is a warning. Remember my formula for change?

New Choices + Consistent Practice = Change

Many of us continue to live as if we have no choices. This keeps us functioning, in part, as children. And when we continue to feel like children, we turn our backs on the priceless privilege of personal choice and slam the door on hope for change.

Now the warning: *proceed with prayer, because more pain is just around the corner.*

I've warned several times about the pain inherent in the change process. We need this caution sign because of how terrifyingly painful it is when we begin practicing some of the suggestions below while laying aside our lifelong self-wounding self-defenses. We made our earliest choices about how to keep ourselves safe and acceptable so long ago that we probably can't remember living any other way. It may even feel as if we and our defenses are one.

These self-protective patterns are not just woven into the fabric of our lives; they seem grafted into the tissue of our beings. We cannot painlessly put them away as childish things without some inner tearing and emotional hemorrhaging. Know this. Believe this. It is true. Still, we must put them away because they are rooted in lies. And we are called to truth.

Healing Self-Inflicted Self-Concept and Perfectionism Wounds

Here are some practical and helpful suggestions for change in these areas of our lives.

1. Learn the difference between self-focus and self-awareness. While an intense, temporary self-focus is almost always necessary to launch the changing process, the goal is a wise, realistic self-awareness. People who lack self-awareness are unnecessarily vulnerable and even dangerous.

2. Begin learning who you really are. God has an unmarred mirror into which we can look to see our true identities (see James 1:22–25). It's the Bible, of course. Use the verses listed in appendix A to get started on your quest for your true identity.

3. Redefine yourself and key people in your life from a more mature and truthful perspective. As you review your childhood realities, you also need to redefine them, because one of the primary characteristics of any abusive system is perpetrator-defined reality. Such distorted presentations of reality cause kids to stumble into distorted thinking patterns that need to be evaluated with our renewed minds (see Romans 12:2). For example, "I am a slut and that's why Daddy had intercourse with me" becomes "I am an incest survivor because my father repeatedly raped me when I was a child."

As healing progresses, you will continually redefine yourself as you reevaluate the events of your childhood in ways that accept them as parts of your personal history without letting them claim the core of your identity.

Healing Self-Inflicted Needs-Denial Wounds

Those who spent their early years in a hurting, hurtful family where little to no emotional nurturing was available survive the pain by learning to deaden and deny their needs. Sadly, many who made that early childhood choice go on thinking that there is no alternative.

Here are some truth-honoring ways to begin respecting your legitimate needs.

1. Learn to identify long-denied needs. Many have survived by giving the significant people in their lives whatever they wanted, and in so doing they never developed the skill of listening to their own needs. This issue arose in an incest survivors group I led.

When Jamie's husband mentioned to his brother how painful Jamie's counseling was for her, the brother-in-law expressed surprise. "She looks pretty healthy to me," he said.

As Jamie and the other incest survivors talked, they realized they all had refined the skill of hiding their neediness. Simultaneously, they perfected the skill of looking happy and making the people around them look good to others and feel good about themselves.

They had become so good at looking good no matter what that they had begun to believe their own disguise. And they had covered their wounds so successfully that people never knew they needed help, let alone offered any. As a result, the women realized that they were hurting themselves by diminishing their support systems of possible helpers. This is another classic example of how we hurt ourselves more by hiding the hurt we have.

2. Purposefully identify and engage your support system, and extend it into a helping network. Here are a few suggestions for getting started: join a group, attend a seminar, or find a church that encourages honest acknowledgment of human struggles and provides help and support in the process. These are great ways to network with other sincerely struggling changers.

3. Begin to see your body as clean from all past abuse. Whether you were the victim, the victimizer, or both, the Bible says, "The blood of Jesus Christ, his [God's] Son, purifies us from all sin" (1 John 1:7).

This verse has been extraordinarily encouraging to me. If "all" doesn't mean every sin, then God is lying. God did not include "all" just to make the print come out even on the page. As I've meditated on God's outrageously inclusive "all," it has expanded even more. If "all" means every possible kind of sin, it is more than just our sins against others. "All" includes others' sins against us. Our bodies, in many cases, were sinned against for years. And some of us have used our bodies to sin against others. Our bodies may have been both the receivers of sin and the conveyers of sin. So, it's just like our awesomely thorough God to include our bodies in the complete cleansing of His dear children.

If you are a survivor or perpetrator of incest, rape, or other hands-on abuse, you need to memorize and meditate on Hebrews 10:22: "Let us draw near to God with a sincere heart and with the full assurance that faith brings, having our hearts sprinkled to cleanse us from a guilty conscience and having our bodies washed with pure water." Please reread that verse. Do you realize what it means? It means that my body has been cleansed from my step-uncle's dirty, degrading sexual abuse. It means the same for each of you, whatever your personal history.

The consequences of years of sins against our bodies do not

disappear just because we give our hearts and lives to Jesus. Nevertheless, in God's sight we are clean in spirit, soul, and body (1 Thessalonians 5:23).

4. Begin treating your body respectfully. This includes proper sleep, exercise, and nutrition. Seek creative and enjoyable ways to do this—especially the exercise part. And don't forget to relax. If you're like me, you probably have a history of relaxation deprivation. If you clear the "right to relax" hurdle, you might consider a real stretch—playing. (Even though *play* is a four-letter word, it is not obscene.)

5. Schedule time for you. I know this means changing your routine. That's the point. Freeing a slice of time for yourself sends a clear message to you and to others that you respect yourself and your healing process. This could mean using the Do Not Disturb feature on your phone or putting your phone away when you want uninterrupted time. An even more shocking possibility is to just let your phone ding without answering the text or notification. It's not against the law.

> **Freeing a slice of time for yourself sends a clear message to you and to others that you respect yourself and your healing process.**

If you have preschool children at home or you work long hours, finding time for yourself is a challenge, to be sure. But don't give up. Try swapping childcare with a friend who also wants some "just for me" time. Use your lunch hour more creatively at work. Find a restful place to be alone with your thoughts and feelings. Read Scripture and pray, close your eyes and daydream, or write in your journal.

Healing Self-Inflicted Emotional Wounds

Continuing to live as if not feeling or showing emotions is the same as not having them is choosing to continue living a lie. What's more, it's a guaranteed way of never experiencing significant healing. For those who are tired of that hurtful way, the following ideas can help you make the turn toward change.

1. Recognize that God gave us emotions, and they are part of how we reflect His character. If you are still afraid of your emotions, review the discussion of Jesus's expression of feelings in chapter 2.

2. Assess your own beliefs about emotions. Use appendix B to think through how different your life would be if you consistently lived according to shame-free and truthful beliefs. Discuss your thoughts with a friend, support group, or counselor. Most importantly, begin putting feet to these truths by making new choices.

3. Find a safe place to feel and appropriately express authentic emotions. This is what individual and group counseling provides, ideally. Healthy Bible study groups may do the same, depending on the intensity of your emotional wounds.

4. Seek help immediately to get free of crippling addictions to things such as alcohol, cocaine or other illegal drugs, and prescription tranquilizers. Don't try to follow a Lone Ranger recovery program. Admitting the problem to others and asking for help is an essential part of healing.

Healing for Self-Inflicted Wounds

We've established the need to keep the idea of process in mind as we work toward changing and healing. Yet while we tighten our seat belts for the lifelong journey, it helps to set some markers along the way to indicate our progress. The Healing Overview and Progress Evaluation (HOPE) chart lists the major issues covered in each chapter along with brief descriptions of three significant stages of recovery, whether from seen or unseen injuries.

Healing for Self-Inflicted Wounds
Healing Overview and Progress Evaluation (HOPE) Chart

Key Issues	Seeing Truth	New Choices	New Practices
Performance-based worth	Seeing what I've been doing to earn the right to be	Letting myself learn who I really am as God sees me	Learning to treat myself with the respect due to all of God's children
Perfectionism	Believing the Bible that all people are flawed	Giving myself the right to be wrong	Learning to accept my flaws without indulging them
Denying my own needs	Realizing I have real human needs	Starting to identify my real human needs	Learning to get my needs met appropriately
Denying my real feelings	Recognizing I have more emotions than those deemed "acceptable"	Giving myself permission to identify real feelings	Learning to express authentic emotions appropriately

Pause to Ponder and Pray

Ponder

Use the HOPE chart to discover where you are in your changing and healing process. Remember, this isn't a contest. Start practicing this new behavior: do not compare yourself and your progress to anyone else. That's tough to avoid if you were motivated in childhood with unfavorable comparisons. Read 2 Corinthians 10:12 to get God's view of such motivation.

Pray

> *Lord, please help me believe you when*
> *you tell me who I am as a child in your*

family. Thank you, Jesus, for being perfect,
because I've tried so hard for so long and
have never been able to be. Amen.

CHAPTER NINE

HELP FOR HEALING
FRIENDS AND SPOUSES

The problem with my friends is that they're all a bunch of sinners. Seriously—every last one.

That's why I fit right in.

As human beings, we are all weak and needy as well as capable and kind. And all the time that we're looking to others to meet our needs, they're looking to us to meet theirs. And of course we fail and then disappoint one another. What a mess!

Human relationships are endless cycles of inflicting and enduring and then tending and grieving our inner wounds. And this cycle will continue apart from divine intervention. In the meantime, reducing the size, depth, and frequency of interpersonal wounding is a reasonable and achievable goal.

New Wounds from Old Patterns

The issues covered in previous chapters are not isolated from one another; they overlap and interact. For instance, if we're perfectionists, we fear failure. Yet one makes the other inevitable. When mistakes or failures draw criticism, a performance-based self-concept takes a tumble. Since we can't tolerate criticism in any form, we react defensively and alienate those close to us. This only reinforces our beliefs that we must be perfect to be accepted.

That example illustrates not only how personal and relational issues interact but also how we wound ourselves and others with the self-protective maneuvers we choose early in life. Again, we face the truth that what we learn in our families shapes every area of our lives.

In the nineties, a landmark study made waves at an American Psychological Association conference and then headlines across the country for validating the idea that unexamined childhood perceptions put women at risk to further abuse. Research with over seven hundred university women demonstrated that those who "experienced rape or attempted rapes as adolescents had a 239 percent greater chance than other women of experiencing rape or attempted rape during the first year in college."[1]

The study also found that women who had experienced family violence or sexual victimization before age fourteen had a 244 percent greater chance of encountering adolescent rape or attempted rape than other women.

I was astounded that my mental health colleagues and the Associated Press were apparently surprised that childhood victimization predisposes people for repeated victimization as adults. To use my husband's expression, "That's a no-brainer." It is merely modern evidence for ancient truth: children can be caused "to stumble" (see Matthew 18:6) into patterns of thought and behavior that have devastating long-term results.

The study's director noted that sexual assault must be addressed in much younger populations of students, such as middle and high schoolers, because "a lot of the damage has already been done by the time these [sexual assault victims] reach adulthood." Indeed, it has. The researchers concluded, "Childhood experiences may affect a child's sense of what healthy relationships are like and encourage behaviors that make them more vulnerable to later assault."

May affect? Where else would we learn about relationships except through childhood experiences? And since our earliest relationships are within families, we naturally assume that our family reflects the way all relationships are supposed to be.

When substantially healthy parents model biblical patterns of relating, they inoculate their children against abusive adult relationships. Unfortunately, boys and girls growing up in hurting and hurtful homes miss learning the basics about healthy relationships.

The Basics of Healthy Relationships

At conferences when I say, "Many of us wouldn't know a healthy relationship if it bit us on the nose," people chuckle. They also nod vigorously in recognition of an uncomfortable truth for most adults raised in hurtful families.

Through the trial and error of tears and years, some of us have learned how to have reasonably healthy relationships. Others are still befuddled by the whole thing.

We've looked at a lot of factors that undermine relationships; now let's examine two that uphold healthy relationships.

Mutual Respect

When two individuals have respect for themselves and for others, they have one-half of the foundation for a healthy relationship. In mutually respectful relationships, we uphold one another's right to individual opinions and choices. We can do this because we respect our own opinions and choices enough that we don't need to have them constantly validated by those around us. Therefore, we don't badger or manipulate others into agreeing with us.

In interpersonal relationships, as in all other areas of our lives, we must operate from truth. This means that we respect others because they bear God's image and are the objects of His love. We complete this truth by remembering that His image in us and in others is marred by sin.[2] Therefore, it is unrealistic, unbiblical, and dangerously naive to expect every person we know to be honest and trustworthy.

Mutual Responsibility

When we balance mutual respect with a realistic understanding of human nature, we won't expect to always admire or agree with everything others do. With this balanced and truthful perspective, we will relate with realistic respect toward ourselves and toward others. And respecting others as much as we respect ourselves means letting other adults take responsibility for the consequences of their choices just as we do for ours.

> Respecting others as much as we respect ourselves means letting other adults take responsibility for the consequences of their choices just as we do for ours.

When mutual respect and responsibility characterize our relationships, we will be safe but not hurt-free. Because we all are human, we will unintentionally wound one another. But this is vastly different from what occurs in unhealthy relationships.

Unhealthy relationships express the self-protective choices we made in response to the three basic questions we faced as youngsters.

Relational Defenses for Answering the Question of Safety

The first question, you may recall, is "Can I be safe?" In a secure family environment, we learn that we can let people get close to us. This doesn't mean, however, that we will want everyone to get close to us. Rather, if we grew up feeling safe, we feel comfortable allowing people into our lives.

When we choose to trust only ourselves to stay safe, we usually operate from one of two extremes: porcupine or octopus.

The people I call porcupines are those who keep themselves safe by keeping others at a distance—a great distance. In contrast, others behave more like an octopus. They enfold, wrap around, cling to, entangle, and entwine their relational tentacles with anyone who comes along.

These relating extremes involve issues of personal boundaries, the sense of where we end and where others begin. Healthy personal boundaries are not completely open and permeable, nor are they closed and impermeable. They do not allow everything and everyone in nor build walls that keep everything and everyone out.

The following chart shows the contrast between these extremes.[3]

Comparing Healthy and Unhealthy Personal Boundaries

Too Permeable Octopus Style	Appropriately Permeable Healthy Style	Impermeable Porcupine Style
I talk at an intimate level at the first meeting. I instantly, totally trust everyone I meet.	I don't overwhelm people with personal information. I allow time for trust to develop.	I don't ever open up, even to people I know to be trustworthy and caring.
I am overwhelmed and preoccupied with a person and his or her needs.	I am able to keep relationships in perspective and function effectively in other areas of my life.	I don't let myself even think about another person I'm interested in.
I can fall in love with a new acquaintance.	I know love is based on respect and trust; these take time to develop.	I don't ever let loving feelings develop with anyone.

Too Permeable Octopus Style	Appropriately Permeable Healthy Style	Impermeable Porcupine Style
I let others determine my reality.	I believe my perceptions are as accurate as anyone's.	I am unwilling to listen to others' perceptions.
I let others direct my life.	I make decisions for myself based on God's leading of my choices.	I refuse to consider the opinions of others.
I don't ever notice when others invade my personal boundaries.	I notice when others try to make decisions for me, are overly helpful, and/or don't consult me about planning my time.	I never allow anyone to help me or give me ideas and suggestions even when it is helpful and appropriate.
I sacrifice my values if necessary to feel close to significant others.	I am not willing to do certain things just to maintain a relationship. I have biblical values that are not negotiable.	I am never willing to change anything I do to please anybody.

Understanding the Extremes

Porcupines, or people who choose over-distancing as a method of staying safe, learned early in life that when people get within range, they fire. Consequently, they learned to stay clear of all close relationships.

Daren is the quintessential porcupine; he doesn't trust anyone. His chaotic and abusive childhood convinced him that trusting anyone and being open at any time would inevitably result in pain. As an adult, Daren uses under-trusting and over-distancing to shield himself from hurt. The only place he feels safe is within himself.

Octopus-type relaters, on the other hand, choose over-trusting and under-distancing as a bridge to safety. They look for safety outside themselves. Touchy-feely, boundary-invading over-trusters seem to believe that a gush of instantaneous total trust—during which they spill their innermost longings and intimate vulnerabilities to strangers—can transform even the most untrustworthy person into a paragon of virtue. "Surely he won't hurt me when he knows how much I trust him," they seem to say. But all the trusting in the world cannot create a trustworthy person, as Amanda learned.

Sobbing convulsively, she told me this story about her sexual relationship with a co-worker. "I just knew the minute I met him that I could trust him completely," she said in what I've come to recognize as a classic octopus statement. This "wise and kind man," as Amanda described him, said he loved her and promised they would marry as soon as he settled some minor personal problems.

Amanda never asked her lover any details about his life or problems because she didn't want him to think she didn't trust him. When Amanda told this man that she was pregnant and would like to get married immediately, you can guess his response. Amanda's "wise and kind" lover laughed and told her that he already had a wife and family and that he had no intention of leaving them. His parting comment to Amanda was "You're too naive for your own good." He was right, sadly.

> When we trust appropriately, we make a reasonable choice based on other people's records of consistent (though imperfect) reliability.

Trusting, Relational Safety, and Intimacy

All human beings long for intimacy, but intimacy is not cheap. Genuine intimacy never develops unless both parties trust that the relationship is psychologically and physically safe. Although we don't always recognize it, trusting always is a choice.

When we trust appropriately, we make a reasonable choice based on other people's records of consistent (though imperfect) reliability. But instead of learning to trust appropriately, under- and over-trusters keep relying on their magical self-protective relational styles to keep them safe. The childhood fantasy that says "I can cause events and control people" is amazingly resilient. Unfortunately, it is amazingly ineffective, and it inevitably causes people to feel more isolated and abandoned, which then confirms their inferior self-concepts and keeps them believing that their imperfections disqualify them from loving relationships.

Answering Identity and Attachment Questions

Can I be me? "Not really" is the conclusion of many from hurtful families. Each of us has strengths and weaknesses, but if I'm shame-bound and believe that I must earn the right to exist and be in a relationship, I might center my identity on always being strong and never showing weakness so I can take care of others.

Here's the logic behind such a choice. If I am shame-wounded, I can't comprehend that any reasonably healthy person would choose to relate to me. But if you are weak and needy, you might be desperate enough to keep me in your life to take care of you. In effect, early identity wounds mean we have to make ourselves indispensable precisely because we believe we're so worthless.

The more we believed as children that we would never earn the right to be close to people or be affirmed for our achievements if anyone suspected we weren't flawless and problem-proof, the more we tend to spend our lives in unbalanced, disrespectful, or even abusive relationships. For example, we might join the ranks of rescuers who function like cosmic mops. They go behind the people they're rescuing and mop up the messes they leave—all the financial, legal, and other kinds of predicaments they create—so they don't have to contend with the consequences of their inappropriate behavior.

When we take this so-called strong position in a relationship, we are saying that the answer to "Can I be accepted?" is "Only if I control the important people and circumstances in my life." Only if, as the needed person, I can feel snugly and securely attached to a needer.

Curiously, some who play the rescuer role endure degrading and even dangerous situations in the name of love. They even attempt to save others they consider poor, helpless victims by trying to control their inappropriate or self-destructive behavior, such as alcoholism.

Ironically, we always end up feeling controlled when we attempt to control others (for their own good, of course). I will be able to appropriately and lovingly detach from you unless I am trying to control your behavior or, especially, your opinion of me. If I'm determined to control either, you can tell me (directly or indirectly) to stand on my head while stacking greased BBs and I'll do it. Your hook to control me, in reality, is my desire to control you.

The truth is that unless I am a prisoner, a hostage, or in some other situation involving physical duress, I—as an unimpaired adult—cannot be your victim. If you are controlling me, I am a volunteer, not a victim. I probably won't recognize that I'm volunteering, but that doesn't change the fact. This is why we must come to the place of recognizing our self-defensive choices. If I don't recognize that I have chosen to play the victim in certain relationships, I won't realize that I can choose a healthier relational style. Instead, I'll continue sacrificing my self-respect and self-control on the altar of controlling others as I live out the fantasy that I can—or should be able to—control other human beings.

In contrast, some adults choose a defensive style, building their identity on being the weak, needy, under-responsible, helpless victim. We may feel relationally safe being the needer—that is, being helpless enough to make any reasonably decent person feel guilty for not helping us. We give up trying to earn anything and settle instead for taking as a way to feel safe and stay connected to all the rescuers who live to give. In effect, we play a victim role in life.

We must clearly understand, however, that children do not play a victim role or freely choose such a relational position. Abused children *are* victims. Sadly, some genuinely victimized children unknowingly choose to remain in the victim role even when they get older and other options are available.

The following chart summarizes the over-responsible, strong rescuer and under-responsible, weak victim styles of relating, contrasted with a more balanced, healthy position.[4]

Personal Responsibility Extremes

Weak Victim Under-Responsible	Healthy Adult Responsible for Self	Strong Rescuer Over-Responsible
I am so weak. I am a wreck.	I have strengths and weaknesses. I am a human being.	I am so strong. I am a rock.
I have no responsibility for anyone or anything.	I am responsible for myself and to others.	I am responsible for everything and everyone.
I can't change anybody.	I can change only myself.	I can change everybody.
I need someone to take care of me all the time.	I can take care of myself most of the time. I trust God to care for me at all times.	I will take care of you all the time.
Everything is too much for me.	Some things are too much for me, but nothing is ever too much for God.	Nothing is too much for me.
I desperately need you.	I desperately need God, and I long for relationships.	I desperately need to be needed.

Children in hurtful families often must be both victim and rescuer. Incest victims typically are forced to rescue their abusers from legal consequences by keeping the incest secret. And if they don't do any healing or changing, they likely will bounce between victim and rescuer roles in the same or different relationships.

Rescuers must have (or create) victims, and victims always need to find rescuers. Both roles are disrespectful and destructive to individuals and relationships. So, what happens if we attempt to move out of those two roles? As sure as night follows day, we get forced into a third.

The Karpman Drama Triangle

The Karpman Drama Triangle was first proposed by psychiatrist Stephen B. Karpman in the 1960s and has since become a useful tool for describing dysfunctional interpersonal interactions. Picture an upside-down triangle with *rescuer* and *persecutor* at the top two corners and *victim* at the bottom corner. These are the only three roles available in unhealthy, unbalanced, and unbiblical relationships. Here's how it would work in a situation involving your use of my credit card.

Rescuer Corner: As long as I continue allowing you to use my credit card, I am keeping you from tasting the sour fruit of your spendthrift lifestyle. And as long as I continue to fill the rescuer corner of the Karpman Drama Triangle, you think I'm kind and generous.

Victim Corner: As I continue to disrespect you by not expecting you to be as responsible for your debts as I am for mine, I might have to find a second job or cut back my spending. Under my breath, I mumble, "Why am I always the one getting hurt when all I want to do is help?" But I say it very softly, of course, so no one hears and concludes that I am unsympathetic—or, worse, selfish. Clearly, I've arrived at the victim corner.

Persecutor Corner: But what if the debt on my credit card is approaching a critical mass no matter how hard I work, and I finally tell you that your free ride is over? You may tell me (and others probably) that I am unsympathetic and judgmental. And there I am—smack-dab in the persecutor position. If my sense of identity, safety, and worth depends on being loved by everyone I meet, I may buckle under the painful pressure of the persecutor role and continue our unbalanced, unhealthy relationship.

This same role shifting occurs when we begin at the victim position. People helpers recognize the classic example of child abuse survivors who decide to stop rescuing their abusers and to start telling the truth. Without fail, abuse-protecting families perceive these courageous truth-telling survivors as persecutors who are stirring up trouble.

Unhealthy relationships doom people to the existence of a Ping-Pong ball bouncing between the role of victim and rescuer. The only way out of that hurtful game is to stop playing it and to risk making the other players angry. Unhealthy relational systems do not include an option of balanced, biblical, mutual "one-anothering."

The New Testament uses the phrase "one another" many times to describe relationships marked by mutuality. For example, "Be kind and compassionate to one another, forgiving each other" (Ephesians 4:32). One-anothering relationships exhibit a healthy balance because both people take responsibility to do what Scripture exhorts. It's not one being kind and forgiving while the other continues being cruel and hurtful.

As I've reflected on the personal and relational qualities necessary for balanced and biblical interactions, I have found the following table helpful. The Wilson Relationship Rectangle shows the interaction of personal responsibility and respect for others in four relational positions.

The Wilson Relationship Rectangle

Respect for Others

		High	Low
Responsibility for Self	**High**	*One-Anothering* "You're worth respecting and being responsible for yourself and so am I."	*Rescuer* "You're a mess and I'm a mop."
	Low	*Volunteer Victim* "You're worth whatever I have to endure from you."	*User-Abuser* "You're a resource and I'm a user."

The user-abuser role in unhealthy adult relationships needs a word of explanation. When hurting and hurtful folks are blatantly abusive (using, for instance, battering fists or words), we can spot them easily or with minimal help. Sometimes, though, their abuse is expressed differently, seemingly harmlessly, but nevertheless selfishly. Although the words and fists are missing, the attitude is clear: "You are a resource for me to use for my purpose and pleasure." People who do this are like the bachelor farmer who advertised for a wife. His ad read, "Man 35 wants woman about 25 with tractor. Send picture of tractor." Some of us keep getting into relationships with people who only want what we have, and then we wonder why we keep feeling used.

The Wilson Relationship Rectangle includes a healthy relational position encompassing both a high degree of personal responsibility and high respect for others. Adopting such a relating style might just alter our entire social lives.

Usually without knowing it, many of us spend our adult years scanning our environments to find people who resemble our earliest and most significant others—parents or other important adults from childhood. Each of these adult life stand-ins offers a "next time," as in, "Next time I'll be lovable enough to make him stay with me forever."

For some spouses, a fifty-fifty relationship means "I dirty, you clean" or "I spend, you earn." Put differently, I choose to be under-responsible, so you must choose to be over-responsible. Whichever responsibility style we choose, it creates problems. And these problems show up most clearly in the most intimate of all relationships—marriage.

The Special Challenges of Marriage

Most of us give more thought to purchasing a new car than to selecting a mate. And the more shame-bound our self-concept is, the more we operate from the attitude that says painful love is better than no love at all. We unknowingly filter out clear signs of potentially hurtful habits, such as jealousy, verbal abuse, unrealistic expectations, hypersensitivity, and blaming others for problems.

We won't even stop to ask ourselves simple, basic questions:

- Am I willing to spend my life with this person if he or she never changes one bit?
- Do I want to become more like this person as she or he is now?
- Do I want this person, just as he or she is now, to be the father or mother of my children?
- Do I want my children to be just like this person as she or he is right now?

These four questions address one of the giant pitfalls of unhealthy marriages. Namely, many of us don't commit to romantic partnerships so much as we contract for renovation projects. We undertake complete overhauls of our spouses before the wedding cake gets stale.

This approach to marriage expresses the shame-bound belief, "You must be perfect because your real role is to prove that I can attract a perfect person, which will keep others from discovering that I'm imperfect." The logic here is that a perfect person would be too smart to marry an imperfect person. But healthy marriages are based not only on mutual, realistic respect and balanced responsibility but also on accepting a spouse as is.

Lexie, a growing, changing thirtysomething daughter of perfectionistic parents told her Christian support group, "When I first started facing my perfectionistic demands on myself, I began to see the impossible stuff I was expecting from my husband. He was always angry, and I was always disappointed and depressed. Lately I've started thinking of him like a great find at an outlet store. I mean, it helps to see him as good but imperfect merchandise that I agreed to take as is. After all, isn't that the way God agreed to take me?"

Indeed, it is. And what's more, God repeatedly and clearly tells us that. We could say that God's agenda for interacting with us is as up front and open as we are able to receive. In contrast, we often hide our agendas.

Hidden Agendas in Marriage

One reason that spouses anger and disappoint us so much and so often is because we keep insisting that they love us unconditionally. They can't, and they never will. It's true that some come closer than others, but no person can do the humanly impossible—rise completely above their own needs and wants in order to totally meet ours. But that's usually the deep desire and hidden agenda many of us carry across the threshold as we enter marriage. Most of the time, however, we hide these desires and agendas—even from ourselves.

All we know is that we have deep, nameless longings and that we expect our unsuspecting spouse to satisfy them. But spouses have their own longings and agendas too. And our vague feeling that something is missing fuels a kind of fill-me-up fantasy.

It's as if we expect marriage to be a long stop at a gas station where each empty spouse assumes the other will do the filling.

With this hidden agenda, both spouses come to the altar and sweetly murmur "I do." But what they really mean is, "I do promise to let you spend every waking moment kissing the painful boo-boos of my life and taking away all my hurts and making me feel better. And if you do, I promise to stay with you."

We can't miss the sad irony of this approach to relationships in general and marriage in particular.

Deep, often unknown longings for personal fulfillment take as many different forms as there are spouses. Similarly, individual agendas differ. One of the most common hidden agendas for spouses raised in hurtful families involves the emotion-laden issue of loyalty.

Hidden Agendas of Divided Loyalty

Many spouses never transfer their primary loyalty from their birth family to the family established by marriage because they never learned that they should or could. This is the "leaving and cleaving" principle of Genesis 2:24, which says spouses (husbands, specifically) are to separate from their parents and inseparably bond to their mates.

> **We can't set appropriate boundaries if we are still attempting to control others' responses to us.**

Hurting and hurtful parents make this essential leaving and cleaving process very difficult. In fact, it becomes impossible if we simultaneously try to maintain our status as loyal children of parents who decide to punish our leaving. We can't set appropriate boundaries if we are still attempting to control others' responses to us.

Michael came from a family that ridiculed him for trying to expand his vocabulary. His parents responded with comments like, "Well, listen to Mr. Big Shot here. I guess he thinks his fancy words make him a whole lot smarter than the rest of us who talk in plain ole English."

To avoid the ridiculing laughter that trailed such comments, Michael learned to live down to his family's expectations.

Neither of Michael's parents finished high school, and both seemed amazed that their son wanted to graduate and go on to the university where he had a full athletic scholarship. Michael met his future wife, Danielle, in college. This is how he describes his struggle with divided loyalties.

> Danielle's folks always encouraged their kids to express themselves to the best of their abilities, and I envied Danielle her great vocabulary. I would never admit that, of course. And I wasn't about to start increasing mine and risk my family's ridicule.
>
> When Danielle used big words around our two sons to help them expand their verbal skills, I ridiculed her in front of them. Wanting to be manly like their dad, they soon learned to belittle both her and articulate speech in general. To this day, both have very limited vocabularies. I would give anything if only I had realized earlier what I was doing to my boys—and to my wife too. I thought I was supposed to live by my parents' values forever, and I was afraid of losing their approval if I didn't. Come to think of it, though, I never felt like I had their approval anyway.

Michael and Danielle eventually sought counseling to strengthen their wobbly marriage, and both worked hard at changing. Both also learned that commitment to their spouse must be placed ahead of commitment to their parents.

Marriage and Ways That Seem Right

Proverbs warns us about the way that "seems right" but that ends in death (14:12 NASB). Many people are still trying to guarantee marital success with ways that seem right. For example, 48 percent of Americans believe that living together before marriage increases the chances for success, while only 13 percent say cohabiting weakens a couple's chance of a successful marriage. (Thirty-eight percent say "it doesn't make much difference.")[5] Researchers have found, however, that cohabiting couples are more likely to separate and divorce.[6]

There are other equally ineffective ways of trying to guarantee marital happiness.

Lauren wears dark glasses and long-sleeved blouses because her husband batters her about once a week. She believes that by taking it she will eventually earn her husband's love and he will stop using her for a punching bag. Lauren doesn't know that all the evidence on spousal battering shows that taking it doesn't stop it, but reporting it might.

In the case of battering, ways that seem right may literally end in death.

I know spouses who have allowed their mates to assault their children to, in their words, "keep the family together." This travesty may seem right, but it is death to the concept of family as God designed it. Parents are responsible for protecting their children until they are adults, even when one spouse must protect them from the other. Some abuse-enabling spouses are more concerned about preserving the family facade than their children's lives.

In a very real sense, divorce is a failure. It produces unforeseen pain and trauma for everyone involved, especially the children. No wonder God says He hates divorce (Malachi 2:16 NASB). And no wonder we lose hope about the prospects for healing our hurting and hurtful relationships. But we don't have to stay in abusive relationships or hurtful patterns. We can make changes, and here are a few ways to begin.

Specific Change Strategies

Remember, change principles apply only to ourselves because *I* am the only person *I* can change. We need this reminder as we look at some specific ways to begin healing relational wounds.

Changing General Relational Patterns

1. Read the New Testament specifically looking for relational principles. Notice especially how Jesus related. Use appendix C to get an idea of how to draw relational principles and personal application from biblical passages.

2. Begin distinguishing between being responsible to *and* for *others.* I am responsible *to* my husband to be a faithful wife. But I am not responsible *for* my husband, his choices, or his behavior. Understanding this difference transforms the quality of our relationship.

> **Change principles apply only to ourselves because *I* am the only person *I* can change.**

3. Practice appropriate trust by using "share, check, share."[7] This is the process of sharing a small part of ourselves and then stopping to check the other person's response. If he or she is respectful and interested, it probably is safe to share a bit more another time. If not, we won't feel totally rejected because we shared only a small part. This strategy helps both under- and over-trusters.

Changing Marital Relating Patterns

1. Apply the general principles of healthy, biblical relating in marriage. It's surprising how often we relate and communicate using helpful principles in the workplace or elsewhere but neglect to take them home with us.

2. Read books, attend seminars, and talk to healthy married couples to learn how you can be a less hurtful and more loving spouse. Did you notice that I am directing you to concentrate on changing *you*? Enough said.

3. Learn to use "I" messages. For example, "I like it when you [do whatever]" or "I feel disrespected when you [do whatever]." This is a helpful, non-blaming way to express appreciation for what our spouses do that we like and to ask for changes in what they do that bothers or hurts us. Of course, even the most respectful, non-blaming communication in the world doesn't guarantee that we'll get what we request.

4. Get help to change abusive patterns in your marriage. Scripture commands us to separate ourselves from "deeds of darkness" and purposefully expose them (Ephesians 5:11). Such deeds include spousal abuse as well as child abuse. You may need to consider separating from your spouse with the goal of working toward reconciliation after significant changes in your relationship. Perhaps an entirely new, healthier foundation needs to be established.

5. Don't pursue divorce until you have worked hard in counseling, exhausted other possibilities, and seen that your spouse intends to repeatedly, unrepentantly desecrate and desert his or her marital commitment. God does not ask you to give your life, or the lives of your children, to rescue your spouse, as dangerously unbiblical Christian counselors and pastors have told some spouses in life-threatening marriages. God sent Jesus to lay down His life to save your spouse. If battering spouses are not moved to repentance by His death, why would they be convinced by your death or your child's? Yes, God hates divorce. But God also hates oppression of the weak. If churches would apply biblical guidelines for disciplining abusive spouses and for helping the victimized as well as the victimizers, there would be far fewer of both.

Healing for Relational Wounds
Healing Overview and Progress Evaluation (HOPE) Chart

Key Issues	Seeing Truth	New Choices	New Practices
Personal boundary styles in relating	I've been too open or too closed as a way of keeping myself safe	Try out a more balanced personal boundary style with my safest friends	Use a more balanced personal boundary style in all my relationships
Personal responsibility styles in relating	I've been using over- or under-responsibility as a defense	Try out a more balanced responsibility style to find those who also seek mutuality	Relate consistently with mutual responsibility and biblical one-anothering
Leaving and cleaving	I haven't transferred primary loyalty from my parents to my spouse	Identify marital problems related to my loyalty conflicts	Consistently put my spouse and his or her needs and desires ahead of my parents'

Pause to Ponder and Pray

Ponder

Use the HOPE chart to get an idea of where you are in your changing and healing process in the area of interpersonal relationships.

You and your spouse can use the Wilson Relationship Rectangle to evaluate your marriage. Share your observations with your spouse after asking him or her to share his or hers with you.

Pray

> *Lord, please help me see and begin making*
> *the changes I need to make to have the kind*
> *of relationships you describe in your Word.*

This is really difficult, so thank you for promising to be all I need to have so that I can do everything you call me to do. Amen.

CHAPTER TEN

HELP FOR HEALING LEADERS

"Don't look back. Something might be gaining on you."
I'd like to change those famous words to "*Do* look back. Someone is following you."

People are following us because all of us are leaders. And all of us are also followers.

Hurt Leaders Hurt More People

We each have a sphere of influence in which we lead. Granted, some spheres are larger and more public than others. Some speak to large audiences while others speak to one preschooler. Whatever our place in life, each of us leads as well as follows.

If all of us are hurting and hurtful people, then, potentially, hurt people with a bigger audience hurt more people.

If the levels of our unseen wounds and power are both high, but our levels of commitment to self-awareness and truthfulness are low, we are extremely dangerous leaders. Perhaps that sounds melodramatic, but it is true. I've seen too many loose-cannon leaders wound too many people. I still have scars from some of them.

Reducing unseen wounds by increasing God-given self-awareness and truth requires difficult, painful change. Sadly, some leaders refuse to undertake it. That's when others with more authority need to intervene to substantially limit such a leader's power and influence. When this happens in business and industry, the result is unemployment. In Christian circles, the result is church discipline.

God knew that churches filled with hurting and hurtful people would need these interventions, so He provided guidelines (see Matthew 18:15–17 and 1 Corinthians 5:1–5). God graciously provides direction for restoration when the repentant leader has experienced genuine healing and change.

Why should we be concerned about the potential of leaders to wound great numbers of people? And why would God put guidelines for church discipline in Scripture? Why doesn't God just call safe, trustworthy, and non-wounding people into leadership roles? (Unfortunately, many followers think He does.)

The reason God uses weak, wounding, needy, hurting, and hurtful people like you and me is because He doesn't have any other kind. There is no other species of humans—at least not on this planet.

The question about our wounds is not, Do we have them? But instead, What are they, where did we get them, and how deep are the scars? When we forget this truth, whether as leaders or as followers, we are dangerous and vulnerable.

The marks of leaders who are likely to hurt followers include, among other things, confusion about authority and approval, conflict about fans or friends and family, and compromise to preserve their place on a pedestal.

Authority Approval Confusion

The more affirmation deprivation children experience, the more intense their approval addiction as adults. As a recovering but frequently relapsing approval addict, I know how powerful this yearning can be. When approval addicts get into leadership positions, they don't shed their emotional baggage like molting snakes shed their skin.

Am I implying that insecure, approval-seeking leaders might pander to their followers rather than risk rejection and the loss of influential positions? Yes, indeed. This issue relates directly to our need for approval and where we seek it when we serve, lead, help, counsel, or minister. It all comes back to whose servants we are.

What's your first impression of this statement? "My ministry is to help and serve people all I can in whatever humble little way the Lord provides." Sound good? Listen again. First, "my ministry" ought to be classified as an oxymoron. But more to the point, this person, by his or her own admission, serves the congregation, church board, and television audience.

There are many reasons for not becoming enslaved to people as an approval-seeking servant. Two stand out. First, we'll burn out faster than you can say "mental breakdown." Consider how pastoral roles have multiplied in recent years. Different folks want their spiritual leaders to do different things. And, since the majority of churches in America have only one full-time pastor, he or she somehow must manage to fill multiple roles.

In large, multi-staff congregations, expectations for leaders can be astonishingly unrealistic and wounding. A friend of mine is a leader in Christian recovery. He is a recovering alcoholic, an ordained minister, a gifted communicator, an effective counselor, and the author of several books. So, it was no surprise when one of Southern California's largest churches contacted him to become their recovery pastor.

To appreciate this story, you have to understand that one of the hallmarks of the recovery movement—Christian or secular—is balanced, healthy living. With that in mind, guess how many hours a week this man was expected to work, as written into the recovery pastor's contract. Fifty. Yes, fifty! While teaching about recovery, he was expected to live a work-focused, unbalanced, and unhealthy lifestyle. If this church had the temerity to write fifty hours a week into his contract, imagine how many unwritten extra hours he would likely have ended up working.

Second, if we serve others primarily, we will look to others primarily for approval. Instead of fixing our eyes on Jesus, as the author of Hebrews tells Christians to do (12:2), we will focus our gaze on others to see how well we're doing.

> If we serve others primarily, we will look to others primarily for approval. Instead of fixing our eyes on Jesus, . . . we will focus our gaze on others to see how well we're doing.

There's a verse tucked away in the Old Testament book of Jeremiah that scores a bull's-eye on this issue. God told His newly called prophet, "Do not be afraid of their faces, for I am with you to deliver you" (1:8 NKJV). I wonder if Jeremiah suffered from approval addiction. God's advice makes me wonder if Jeremiah was scrutinizing faces for the tiniest nuances of disagreement or disapproval so that he could adjust his appearance, words, or whatever it would take to get back into the chilling warmth of hard-earned nods and smiles. I'm speculating, of course. But I understand the fear of faces.

A few years ago, God used John 12:43 to convict me about the depth of my approval addiction. The verse accuses the religious leaders of Jesus's day of loving the approval of other people more than the approval of God. When I read it, I felt as if I'd taken a bullet to the heart. Actually, it was "the sword of the Spirit" (Ephesians 6:17), God's Word, which cut to the heart of a problem in my life—my inordinate desire for affirmation from others.

When our identity and sense of worth depend on other people's approval, we will listen to their words more than to

God's Word. And we may fail to notice how often we choose fans over family and friends.

Friends and Family, or Fans?

Christian counselor Tom Barrett worked in Washington, DC, with a lot of government officials. His observations about their public-life versus private-life struggles apply to many unofficial types as well. Tom noticed that many public-focused people seemed to want fans more than friends, respect more than relationships, and influence more than intimacy.[1]

The independent ministries and Christian businesses that have multiplied in recent decades have created spaces where such a preference for unreal, superficial interactions abounds.

Mark is an evangelical ex-entrepreneur who knows about this firsthand.

"I really thought I was hustling for the Lord, you know. I mean, people poured into my conferences, bought my books, and told me I was great. The tighter my schedule and the greater my responsibilities, the more new people I met who almost always thought I was great. I never bothered to put together a board of directors or connect with a church to provide any sort of oversight. I didn't want anyone getting too close or too involved in my ministry."

Little by little, Mark started to rely on approval as his "standard stuff," as he called it. And little by little, his spiritual and moral life went down the tubes.

As a refugee from a hurtful family, Mark preferred a bump-and-run relational style that never let anyone get too close. Candidly sharing his struggles or seeking honest opinions never made it onto Mark's list of priorities. And he made the same mistake that many make: he confused popular success and a larger bank balance with divine blessing. It's easy to forget that God is the one we are to please, not the paying audience or our public accountants.

Many of us hurting and hurtful people need to ask God to search our hearts and show us if we value fans over friends. Do we keep people at a distance, like fans, or let people get close enough to see our flaws, like friends? We can find the answer to that question in the wisdom found in the hidden parts of our lives (see Psalm 51:6). Or we could ask someone in our family—a spouse, for example—for an honest answer. If we prefer impersonal relationships with adoring fans, this has enormous effects on our families.

> Do we keep people at a distance, like fans, or let people get close enough to see our flaws, like friends?

We don't have to be pastors, government officials, bosses, or famous in any way to be wrestling with a preference for public life. Stay-at-home parents who get involved in church or community volunteer work are just as likely to find their identities in public activities as are prominent leaders.

The more performance-based our self-concepts, the more we tend to focus on high-profile activities (whether paid or volunteer). And let's face it, most at-home stuff is low profile from the world's viewpoint.

Here's my summary of Tom Barrett's observations about the public-life versus home-life struggle.

Public-Life versus Home-Life Conflict

In Public	At Home
I'm treated like Superman.	I'm treated like ordinary Clark Kent.
People are sensitive to my needs.	People expect me to be sensitive to their needs.
I'm expected to help change the world.	I'm expected to change light bulbs, diapers, etc.

Barrett has suggested that if public-performance-focused spouses and parents actually put their families' unwritten contracts in print, they would include some of the following items.

Public Performer's Family Contract

- We understand that I and my public performance are more important than anyone or anything else in this family.
- We understand that I will be preoccupied with giving my all to my public performance.
- We understand that I need to hear your support but not your struggles.
- We understand that I cannot be there for you.
- We understand that all of you are essentially on your own.
- We understand that you are expected to totally deny all of your personal needs.

_____   _____

Signatures: (Husband)   (Wife)

_____   _____

Signatures: (Child)   (Child)

What happens to people with a performance orientation that makes them favor fans over friends and family? I expect the answer is a little different in each situation. But I see a common thread woven through all these hurting folks and their hurting families. The public person is seduced by life on the pedestal.

Preserving a Place on a Pedestal

I use the word *pedestal* to mean a place of leadership where we can create the appearance of being perfect and problem-free.

Pedestals are precarious places for human beings to be because God never designed us to live there. When we cooperate with those who help us get there, we are colluding in fraud, which is a crime legally as well as spiritually.

Shame-wounded adults often gravitate toward pedestals because they believe they must be perfect to earn a place on this planet. As leaders, they don't let others get close enough to notice that they are not perfect. And there are always plenty of other shame-wounded people expecting leaders to be perfect who are happy to go along with the deceit. However, since human beings are not perfect, leaders on pedestals must master some tricky moves to keep anyone from discovering their flaws. This means that pedestal-seeking people inevitably compromise the truth and develop secret lives.

The Secret-Life Syndrome

Unfortunately, stories of high-profile pastors and Bible teachers who have developed secret lives of sexual gratification, bullying and rage, and image-obsessed manipulation have become commonplace. While they looked like upstanding ministry leaders for years, they were caught in the secret-life syndrome.

These pastors are some of the many public figures who have been trapped in the devastating double bind of trying to live on a pedestal. Few of these wounded and wounding leaders started out to live secret lives, but that was the inevitable result when they took the first step up to the seemingly safe "high" place.

For example, if a man habitually visits pornography sites and prostitutes, he probably loathes himself for this and vows each time to try harder to stop. I've even heard of people going into religious work so they would have to stop some despised but life-dominating sin. By preaching and teaching against such behavior, and by knowing the need to model godly living, they hope to paint themselves into a moral corner. After all, everyone will be looking up to them as a perfect example, so they will have to try harder to be perfect.

Apparently these deluded leaders trust other people's expectations to control their out-of-control behavior. This is just another variation on the theme of magical thinking. And because magical thinking denies reality, it always leads to more hurt, not less. The painful part of the double bind is that because these leaders believe they cannot admit the truth about their imperfect and out-of-control lives, they can't reach out and get help. They are trapped on wobbly pedestals, unable to climb down, and must make increasingly desperate attempts to keep from crashing.

Trust Bandits and Sexual Misconduct

Collecting accurate data on pastoral abuse is difficult, of course, but surveys suggest that between 15 and 40 percent of ministers across denominations self-report sexually inappropriate behavior.[2]

When ministers become sexually involved with congregants who come to them for pastoral counseling, the betrayal of trust is devastating beyond description.

Some argue, "But they were adult women, not girls. They're just as responsible for what happened as the minister." Although that may seem like a reasonable evaluation of the situation, and although women in churches are frequently blamed for seducing the pastor, such a conclusion ignores a significant part of the equation: the woman went to the pastor for help.

Writing on this subject, pastor David Johnson and counselor Jeff VanVonderen have this to say: "Even if she did try to seduce him, while that would have been immoral, what he did was illegal. Her behavior would not justify his. There is no legal reason for a pastor to become sexually involved with a counselee. *Someone* is supposed to be the healthy person: Shouldn't it be the spiritual helper?"[3]

Because hurtful spiritual leaders represent God, their immoral and illegal behavior is blatant spiritual abuse. But when these leaders are in large and financially successful churches, such abuse may go unnoticed by all but the victims.

Success and Secrets

In successful organizations—religious or otherwise—small inner circles of people, who either ignore or suppress the truth, surround the leader to perform damage control when the secrets begin to leak.

It's as if sexual abuse and tax evasion don't matter as long as nobody finds out, public messaging remains positive, and generous donations keep coming in.

Leaders with secret lives and secret-supporting organizations understand the power of words to create realities as well as to convey them.

Proverbs 18:21 describes the influence of words when it says that "the tongue has the power of life and death." The Bible describes corrupt leaders as "those who call evil good and good evil" (Isaiah 5:20). No wonder untrustworthy, truth-twisting leaders cause such deep and devastating wounds with their lies and betrayal.

> **If you have to lie about it, don't do it.**

Wilson's Law of Behavior Selection says, "If you have to lie about it, don't do it." Obedience to this law would prevent mountains of misery for millions of followers—and their leaders too. As the Bible says, truth makes us free (John 8:32)—but first it makes us angry and miserable.

To long for the eradication of sin and the blissful, perfect peace that would result is a natural human desire. But to believe that we have arrived at that longed-for state is self-deception. And self-deceived people in positions of leadership are dangerous and hurtful.

The Antidote of Humble Self-Suspicion

In *Rediscovering Holiness*, J. I. Packer uses the phrase "humble self-suspicion" to describe the cure for skewed views of spirituality.[4] Packer believes that many sincere believers are too quick to testify to being wholly holy and spiritually well. He suggests that the spiritual health we proclaim is partial and relative when measured by the absolute standard of spiritual health we see in Jesus.

By all means, let's give God glory because we are less spiritually sick and incapacitated today than we were yesterday. But let's also be honest. This means staying off pedestals, small or large; it means repeatedly telling the truth about our flaws, failures, and ongoing struggles as we attempt to live authentically for Christ. This also means remaining humbly self-suspicious as well as honestly self-aware. We ought to anticipate, rather than be shocked by, our desire to climb onto a pedestal and receive the acclaim of admiring friends, who too quickly can become adoring followers. The more we recognize our susceptibility to such seductive circumstances, the safer and more trustworthy we are, whatever our spheres of influence.

What is the secret to keeping our balance and being less hurtful leaders? It is knowing that the greatest danger for all of us is forgetting that all of us have limitations and are still imperfect and sinful. Dr. Archibald Hart says it this way: "Christian leaders don't fall because they forget they are holy; they fall because they forget they are human."[5]

> The greatest danger for all of us is forgetting that all of us have limitations and are still imperfect and sinful.

Specific Change Strategies

Again, we may need to remind ourselves that we are all leaders to someone, as unlikely as that may seem to some of us. So the following ideas can benefit all of us.

1. Honestly assess the level of binding shame in your belief system. When we function from a shame mindset, we are vulnerable to becoming the kind of leader we've examined.

When we're shame-bound, we'll always feel as if we have to work twice as hard to be half as good as someone else. When we believe that we don't deserve our leadership positions—especially in Christian ministry—we may actually sabotage them without realizing it. Remember, everything about our Christian pilgrimage is God's undeserved grace. Accept whatever place of service God gives you with humility and gratitude.

2. Take time to rest. Leaders on the edge of burnout—whether stay-at-home parents or pastors—usually spend too much time and emotional energy caring for others and too little for themselves. At times, I've felt too tired for a mere coffee break; I needed a psychotic break! That happens when we attempt to outwork and under-rest everyone we know, including Jesus. In the only gospel written by a physician, we read, "Yet the news about him spread all the more, so that crowds of people came to hear him and to be healed of their sicknesses. But Jesus often withdrew to lonely places and prayed" (Luke 5:15–16).

Did you catch the words "often withdrew"? I doubt that Jesus would be hired by a lot of churches if His work habits were widely known. Sometimes we who talk the most about Jesus as our supreme example are the least likely to follow His example of withdrawing to a lonely place to pray.

3. Evaluate your potential for climbing onto a pedestal and crashing into a life of secrecy. If, like me, you struggle with approval addiction, face the fact that you may crave adoration to compensate for your childhood deprivation. When this is the case, we tend to seek followers and fans who see us as more than we are, or ever can be, instead of friends who know us warts and all. This is dangerous and destructive for us and for them.

4. Develop a circle of safe, trusted friends for accountability. I will go so far as to say that without implementing this fourth strategy, it is doubtful whether we can consistently practice the others.

Accountability is an absolute, nonnegotiable must for everyone in ministry of any kind at any level. Period. And it is nearly that critical for the rest of us. At least two or three ruthlessly honest folks who love us a lot and Jesus far more are just what we need for these accountability circles of safety. Such relationships help us flee temptations (sexual and otherwise) and avoid self-deception about our capacity to do and be everything for everyone.

Healing for Leaders' Wounds
Healing Overview and Progress Evaluation (HOPE) Chart

Key Issues	Seeing Truth	New Choices	New Practices
Seeking approval from God, not others	I've been living more for the approval of people than for God's approval	Choosing what I do and say to please God, even when it's not popular	Putting more God-pleasing choices in more areas of my life
Having family and friends, not fans and followers	I prefer high-profile positions that make me feel big	Purposely taking off-the-pedestal positions more often	Being comfortable in both low- and high-profile roles
Accountability to avoid secret-life syndrome	I am at risk for secret-life syndrome	Identifying and engaging the people who can provide accountability	Meeting often and being real with my accountability group

Pause to Ponder and Pray

Pause

Use the HOPE chart to get an idea of where you are in your changing and healing process as a leader.

Review appendix A to remind yourself of your identity in

Christ. The more we believe what God believes about us, the less we'll need to pander for approval and posture on pedestals.

Pray

Lord, help me hold with an open hand and a heart of gratitude whatever positions of leadership you've given me. And please help me keep my eyes on you as I lead. Amen.

CHAPTER ELEVEN

HELP FOR HEALING FOLLOWERS

"I can hardly wait to see what I'll be when I grow up."

My delayed adolescence, which began in my mid-thirties, was due in part to my reluctance to stop viewing leaders as people on pedestals. In my gullible days, I skipped and giggled my way through relationships with people in authority. My husband used to say that I lived in a Sunday-school world because I assumed that everyone was kind, honest, sweet, and sincere. I wore my naivete like a shiny badge of honor and thought he was terribly cynical. Well, my badge tarnished quite some time ago. And I now think that Garth was much closer to the truth than I was.

As followers, we must not only maintain self-awareness and "humble self-suspicion"[1] regarding ourselves, but we need to cultivate a similar approach to others, including leaders. Sound too cynical and unchristian? Read this: "Dear friends, do not believe every spirit, but test the spirits to see whether they are from God, because many false prophets have gone out into the world" (1 John 4:1).

This is God's call to ruthless realism regarding spiritual leaders. He does not want us to swallow everything we hear from every person who claims to represent Jesus Christ. Why then are we so often drawn to doing that very thing?

Often it has to do with gullibility training in hurtful families, where hurtful leaders wear deceitful disguises. Hurting and hurtful families are like prep schools for unhealthy organizations—secular or religious.

Set Up for Follower Wounds

Children growing up in hurting families become champion secret keepers and people pleasers. After all, family rules teach children to accept the leaders' (that is, parents') views of reality without looking at or talking about more truthful views. So, adult children from hurtful families usually have only a vague idea of what constitutes appropriate relationships.

Discussing the fact that churches are beginning to be more conscious of personal boundary issues, a professor at a Midwestern seminary says: "Churches are so much [more] aware of the violations of boundaries, especially with regard to sexual boundaries, that this has created all kinds of havoc and confusion. It reveals that there are many people who, because of the family of origin or whatever, simply are not clear about what's appropriate and inappropriate."[2]

> Stories of deception, institutional cover-ups, spiritual betrayal, and abuses of power remind us why God said to test the spirits of those in authority.

As we learn more about healthy relationships and personal boundaries, we are better prepared to evaluate people's attitudes and actions. Too often, though, wounded followers get rewounded because the magnitude of deception is beyond their comprehension.

Stories of deception, institutional cover-ups, spiritual betrayal, and abuses of power remind us why God said to test the spirits of those in authority. This admonition is easily overlooked, however, when the authority is the person we long to receive approval from.

Authority-Figure Approval Addiction

I've already referred to myself as a recovering approval addict who relapses regularly. Only in the past few years, however, have I recognized that my addiction centers on winning the approval of men in positions of perceived authority. I'm embarrassed that it took me so long to see this when it makes so much sense. Since I never had a healthy male authority figure, I came into adulthood ripe for this addiction.

What's yours? From whom do you most long to win a smile? It may seem simplistic, but approval addictions have a lot to do with our early relationships with our parents. This problem is becoming increasingly prevalent due to the increasing phenomenon known as father loss.

Many adults labeled workaholic are killing themselves and sacrificing their families in the process. For many, the motivation is not a fatter paycheck, bigger office, or higher title; it's approval from male bosses. These employers are like surrogate fathers to adults with severe father hunger. When this happens, the father-starved workers, whether in secular or religious organizations, are at risk for authority abuse.

If you identify with the following sentiments, you may be suffering from approval addiction:

- I am killing myself doing the impossible for the ungrateful.
- I've done so much with so little for so long that I am now qualified to do anything with nothing.

Addiction to the approval of authority figures breeds a love for human approval that surpasses the love for God's approval.

You'll remember from the previous chapter that this was Scripture's scathing indictment of the religious leaders of Jesus's day (John 12:42–43). And they, by the way, loved to make disciples.

Whose Disciples?

Wounded and empty adolescents and adults often turn to appealing and powerful leaders to find fulfillment. This phenomenon fuels religious groups from evangelical churches to outright cults.

During the Great Chinese Famine, some desperate people ate a type of edible soil called kaolin to try to satisfy their hunger. But because the soil contained no nutrients, those who ate the soil eventually starved to death.[3] Those who seek approval from authority figures are the spiritual equivalent of those who eat food with no nutrients. Only Jesus, the "bread of life," can fill hungry hearts and empty lives (John 6:48–51). Jesus calls us to be true disciples (that is, learners), and He promises to fully satisfy all who follow Him. But sometimes, instead of becoming disciples of our Lord, we become disciples of disciples.

God no longer uses other people as go-betweens, as He did before Jesus came to become our "mediator" (1 Timothy 2:5). Shame-bound spiritual seekers struggle with this truth because we can't believe God would ever deal with us directly and personally in Jesus. So we attach ourselves to some person we think is good enough to merit such a direct and personal connection to deity. We try to stay close enough to catch some of the spiritual crumbs that fall from the table of this seemingly special disciple. Unfortunately, some of these leaders dispense terribly toxic spiritual teaching.

Whose Truth?

Some of us may be following spiritual leaders dispensing so-called truths that are dangerous or even absurd when viewed by the clear light of Scripture. But in truth-fearing organizations, the person who sees and describes the problem always becomes the problem. "Why do you want to cause trouble?" is a classic question that leaders in abusive, secret-supporting systems ask when they are threatened by the truth.

This happens in churches too. Many abusive, truth-fearing churches imply that being nice is better than being honest. They're wrong. "Nice" is not even listed among the fruit of the Spirit in Galatians 5:22–23! That's a real shocker to some Christians. It was to Claudia.

> **In truth-fearing organizations, the person who sees and describes the problem always becomes the problem.**

I met Claudia at a conference in California, where she told me her story about changing churches after years of soul-searching and prayer. "Every time I tried to talk to any leaders or staff members about my concern over what I saw in the youth program, I was told to 'think on things that are kind and lovely.' I heard that passage of Philippians quoted so often, I decided I'd better go before the Lord with it and ask for guidance."

Claudia did just that and discovered that the Scripture fragment being used to squelch her concerns was also being twisted to suit the purposes of the church staff. Philippians 4:8 actually begins, "Finally, brothers and sisters, whatever is true . . ." Then it lists other qualities, such as "noble," "admirable," and "excellent," before exhorting believers to "think about such things."

The staff at Claudia's church overlooked the very first thing God wants us to think about—truth.

Six months after she left the church, one of the youth pastors was dismissed and subsequently charged with sexual misconduct with a minor.

Sometimes, however, the shepherds, not the sheep, are the ones being battered and bloodied. I know of church boards who have abused struggling pastors when they tried to walk in truth. When one pastor acknowledged personal and church problems and wanted to get help, the elder board ordered him to resign and threatened to withhold severance pay unless he left quietly, saying he would split the church or cause problems if he told the truth. These elders forgot that "truth is *never* the problem; the problem is *always* the problem."[4]

In other churches, sexually abusing leaders have been quietly transferred to other unsuspecting congregations, while the courageous whistleblower is browbeaten into silence.

Even more evil, perhaps, are churches where sexually abusing leaders hide behind perversions of Scripture, such as "touch not God's anointed" (see Psalm 105:15), while accusing their truth-telling victims of being seductive and stirring up strife. In such unhealthy and unholy situations, the abuser usually remains in his position of trust, influence, and authority while the victim is removed from membership or fellowship.

> **Lovers of truth pay a price in truth-fearing groups.**

Be warned: Lovers of truth pay a price in truth-fearing groups. If truth-noticing followers question their religious leaders' conduct, they often are accused of being judgmental. In the confusion about individual rights, the responsibility for evaluating the behavior of others is sacrificed on the altar of unlimited tolerance and indiscriminate compassion.

We live in a society where tolerance has become more prized than truth or individual responsibility. Tragically, some religious systems hold the same unbiblical values. (See Revelation 2:20 for Jesus's reaction to the tolerance of teaching that departs from truth.) In truthless religious systems, followers who see and speak truth may be told they don't know enough, which means they have no business questioning the leader's doctrines or directions.

John, the beloved disciple, wrote that every Christian has

the same divine anointing that enables us to learn from God, so none of us needs to depend totally on human teachers for spiritual truth (1 John 2:27). God doesn't expect any of His followers to shift our brains into neutral and coast while others steer our spiritual lives.

Where's the Exit?

If we get into one of these unhealthy, power-abusing religious systems because we feel so at home there, is there a way out? Yes, but the cost of getting out is usually enormous pain. Unhealthy religious families often call those who leave apostate or heretical. So, those getting out will probably need to restructure their social lives as well as their spiritual lives if a cultlike religious group is dominating them.

When the secret life of a leader in an unhealthy religious system comes to light, occasionally the leader will repent. Even then, be discerning and test the spirit of the repentant person (see 1 John 4:1).

Where's the Repentance?

When leaders who have hurt us by betraying our trust acknowledge personal wrongdoing and sin, it's wise to evaluate the location of their repentance. With unswerving consistency, God focuses His attention on our inner lives, and His attitude toward repentance is no exception.

Scripture describes two types of repentance, or admission of sin, both mentioned in Joel 2:13:

> Rend your heart
>   and not your garments.
> Return to the LORD your God,
>   for he is gracious and compassionate,

slow to anger and abounding in love,
and he relents from sending calamity.

One type of repentance is to "rend your heart." The other kind is to rend "your garments." The first is a personal, internal response seen only by God and the one who is repenting. In contrast, the second is a public, external demonstration seen by dozens or, these days, even millions of other people.

We can probably all name well-known church leaders who made a public declaration of repentance, only to be later caught or convicted for the same abuses. However, I am glad to say that some leaders have sincerely repented of sexual and other sins, sought and received help, and demonstrated the genuine fruit of repentance that Scripture describes (see Matthew 3:8). We need to know about these cases, otherwise we will become hopelessly disillusioned and give up on church and religious organizations all together, an alternative that is no better than blind, mindless naivete.

What is the secret to walking the tightrope between gullibility and cynicism? It is realizing that the greatest danger is forgetting that all of us are imperfect, sinful human beings, and knowing that God mysteriously works through such imperfect beings. Holding these realities before us keeps us living in balanced interdependence with one another and total dependence on Christ. And that's healthy for leaders and followers alike.

Specific Change Strategies

Anyone who has been wounded in secular or religious organizations is likely to be angry at themselves for being taken in. They may think or even call themselves stupid for it. This response only multiplies the pain with self-inflicted wounds. Instead, try the following suggestions.

1. Get help. Often we can't recognize the progressive steps that led us to follow a leader or serve a boss in an organization that is unhealthy and unbiblical. Some gentle and godly counsel helps enormously as we try to understand the vulnerability that made us so undiscerning.

2. Accept that you are only human. Human beings get tricked, conned, duped, and deceived all the time, especially if in early life they were schooled to close their eyes and ears to contradicting realities. Find a Christ-centered support group for adult children from hurtful families where you can safely share your pain. If you do, you'll hear others describe similar experiences of being deceived by authority figures. It's always comforting to know we're not alone.

3. Learn the biblical marks of an authentic, trustworthy leader. Read the Gospels, looking specifically at Jesus's leadership style. Although the apostle Paul was far from perfect, we can also learn from his leadership qualities described in the Epistles.

God told the prophet Amos that He was going to set a plumb line in the midst of His people (Amos 7:7–8). Anyone who has put up wallpaper knows the value of a plumb line—a weighted piece of string that gives a true vertical line. God's Word is the only trustworthy plumb line of truth in our "warped and crooked generation" (Philippians 2:15). We must use it to make sure the teaching of every leader lines up with God's true vertical.

4. Give yourself permission to grieve lost relationships. The trauma of leaving hurtful groups and leaders is very real and very painful. We must allow ourselves to mourn the relationships that meant so much despite how unbalanced and unhealthy they might have been. We

> **The trauma of leaving hurtful groups and leaders is very real and very painful. We must allow ourselves to mourn the relationships that meant so much despite how unbalanced and unhealthy they might have been.**

need to find healthy helpers to provide support and encouragement during such times.

When we've been deeply wounded in childhood and again in adult life by authority figures, we usually need help to move through our pain into healing. Part of this process probably will include acknowledging that some of our present emotional anguish stems from the emotions we had in childhood but didn't have the freedom to feel or express.

This combination of old and new grief can feel overwhelming. So, at the risk of sounding annoyingly redundant, let me say it again: please get help. Remember, getting help doesn't mean you're weak; it means you're human. And human is how God created all of us.

Healing for Followers' Wounds
Healing Overview and Progress Evaluation (HOPE) Chart

Key Issue	Seeing Truth	New Choice	New Practice
Testing all that leaders say and teach	I am set up to believe all that leaders teach	Give myself permission to question and test all that leaders teach	Test all that leaders teach by comparing it to the Bible

Pause to Ponder and Pray

Use the HOPE chart to get an idea of where you are in your changing and healing process as a follower.

Ponder

- After reading this chapter, do you suspect that you may be in a truth-fearing organization?
- Is there a truth-seeking, trustworthy person outside of this organization you can discuss the situation with?

- If so, will you contact him or her to schedule a discussion? When?

Pray

> *Lord, help me be willing to see the truth about the religious and secular leaders I've believed and followed. If necessary, please give me the courage to leave whatever group I'm in that misrepresents truth. Thank you for your Word, which provides the plumb line against which to measure all teachings. Amen.*

CHAPTER TWELVE

HELP FOR HURTING WORSHIPERS

When surveyed, here's how several middle schoolers described God:

"God is like Santa Claus; everyone knows about him but not everyone believes in him."

"God brings special gifts to good people and tries to help the bad people."

"God is the apple on the tree of life."[1]

These descriptions of God came from twelve- and thirteen-year-olds. In another sense, however, they came from their parents.

Most of us realize by now that our concepts of God are related directly to the kind of relationships we had with our earliest adult authority figures. We don't have to be theologians to figure out that this spells trouble for children raised in hurting and hurtful families. Actually, it spells spiritual abuse.

All child abuse is spiritual abuse. Mistreating children through neglect or blatant abuse misrepresents the character and purposes of God, the ultimate authority figure. And that creates confusion about God that can last a lifetime.

Confusion about God

We don't have to be beaten, sexually abused, locked in closets, or abandoned on someone's doorstep to have distorted ideas about God.

"I came from a faithfully churchgoing home," said Josh, a young would-be seminarian. He then described being raised by a morally clean, hardworking, rigidly religious, demanding father and a passive, manipulative mother. The youngest of five children, Josh learned at age six that he was an unwanted accident when he overheard his mother say that to her sister.

"That was the moment when I determined to make my mom and dad happy they had me," Josh said. "But no matter how hard I tried, I've never really felt like I was good enough or did enough well enough to do that."

Josh sought counseling because of what he heard me say in a seminar at our church. Specifically, he was concerned about entering seminary with his views of God as they were.

"I was so surprised when you said that God is not disappointed with us even though He's grieved about our sins," Josh told me. "See, my problem isn't so much horrible sinning. Sure, I know I fail all the time, and I confess it. But the thing that bothers me most is that I always feel like God is really disappointed in me. Like, my quiet times—they're never good enough somehow."

As I gently probed for how this idea of God's disappointment affected him, Josh's eyes began to glisten.

"I really know that I trusted Jesus as my Savior, but I just keep wondering if I was supposed to. I know that sounds stupid. But I just keep wondering if God accepts that I'm His child even though I can't do everything as good as I wish I could."

I've met a lot of Joshes through the years, because many Christians never feel good enough to be accepted and loved by God. In effect, they all worship a disappointed God.

Worshiper Wounds from Being Treated as Special

Anyone raised by imperfect parents (which everyone was) has a somewhat distorted view of God. Our job as adults is to correct the distortion by learning the truth about God. My distorted deity was a demanding God.

For most of my life I worshiped a deity who was never fully pleased with what I did because He expected more from me than from His other children.

Like many well-meaning Christian parents, my mother used scriptural support for her perfectionistic expectations of me. I can still hear her quoting the portion of Luke 12:48 that says, "From everyone who has been given much, much will be demanded." That verse stirred a sense of gratitude for being "given much" while it generated guilt, because no matter how much I did or how well I did it, much more seemed to be required. I grew up loving both God and my mother because they had given me so much. At the same time, I feared that I constantly disappointed them both because I could never fully satisfy their demands.

The year before she died of cancer at age seventy-eight, my mother told me several times that she felt guilty for depriving me of a father.

When I was a child, my mother tried to show me that even though I didn't have an earthly father to love me, my heavenly Father proved that He loved me by giving me special gifts, like playing the piano, singing, and speaking in public. She did this not only because she sincerely loved me but also, I believe, because it soothed her wounded conscience to believe that she bore a special child.

And perhaps she saw her supposedly special child—me—as a sign that God was not angry about her failed first marriage.

Ironically, my mother was correct about how important earthly fathers are to children learning about their heavenly Father.

Father Wounds and Spiritual Confusion

Simply stated, the way our parents—especially our fathers—treat us in childhood molds the concepts that shape our relationship with God. We see evidence of such a connection in our worship lives.

In your journal or on your phone, briefly answer the following questions about your father or the person(s) who filled the father role in your childhood.[2]

> The way our parents—especially our fathers—treat us in childhood molds the concepts that shape our relationship with God.

1. How close were you to your father? How approachable was he?
2. Did he show you that you were intrinsically valuable and unconditionally loved, or did you have to perform to earn value and love?
3. Did he have time for you? Were you important enough to him to get his appropriate attention? (Sometimes when fathers or parents spend time with their children, it is inappropriate and hurtful. For instance, it is inappropriate for your father to spend time with you for his sexual gratification or as an excuse to get out of the house so he can drink.)
4. Did he keep his promises? Was he trustworthy?
5. Were you punished for being bad or disciplined for character improvement?

Now answer the same questions about God. For example, "How close am I to God? How approachable is He?" When you finish answering the second set of questions, compare your responses. Are there similarities? Most likely there are, because fathers are such powerful influences in their children's lives.

Fathers create their daughters' expectations about relationships with men in general, and they model for their sons what it means to be masculine. As if that weren't enough responsibility, fathers—even more than mothers—also create expectations in their children about the treatment they will receive from God.

Perhaps this is why the messages from our heavenly Parent to earthly parents in Scripture are often addressed to fathers (see Ephesians 6:4 and Colossians 3:21). Fathers cannot avoid this role. Even when they abandon their children or fail to maintain contact after divorce, they are performing this function, though in a negative way. These phantom fathers predispose their daughters to expect desertion by men, while their sons learn that when the going gets tough, real men get going—right out the door. And these absentee dads teach their children that God will abandon them just when they need Him most.

No dad is perfect, but all dads need to be consistently adequate. When children are beaten, raped, humiliated, rejected, and given only performance-based approval, we shouldn't be surprised that they believe God will abuse and reject them too. How could they feel comfortable with someone they think has an ever-lengthening list of demands they must fulfill before He'll accept them? How could they enjoy being with someone they think has a club He's eagerly waiting to use?

The Oxymoron Effect

Fathers who neglect and abuse their offspring create what I call the *oxymoron effect*. An oxymoron is a combination of words that seem to contradict one another—like "fresh frozen." We encounter the oxymoron effect when biblical descriptions of God contradict our experience.

The Bible speaks of God as a loving Father. We grasp the concept of "loving," and we understand the meaning of "father." But if our early experiences with a father figure were unloving, those two concepts seem contradictory, and they cause spiritual confusion.

Counseling clients and others have described this phenomenon in words like these: "I just can't seem to connect to God the way other Christians do. When I hear people pray to or talk about God as a loving father, something inside me freaks out. I want to jump up and scream, 'You've got to be kidding.'"

Women in this situation sometimes join groups that advocate for changes to hymnals and translations of the Bible that use predominantly male images and pronouns in reference to God and God's children. Listen to how such references affected a wounded worshiper named Emily.

> I don't know why, but I've always cringed inside when I uttered the words "Our Father" at the start of the Lord's Prayer. I certainly wish Jesus had picked some term other than "Father" to refer to God. And why are we daughters left out in the Bible? It's as if God prefers males, just like my dad who thinks only he and my brothers are really valuable. My mom, my sister, and I are little better than the family dog. Even Leo, our dog, is male, so he probably ranks ahead of us too.

I wonder if Emily and others like her in the church are reacting to deep father wounds. If so, it helps to explain why some theologically conservative evangelical women join the ranks of their more liberal sisters on these issues.

Everyone has different reasons for adopting theological views, but I am certain of one thing: all of these reasons and views are affected by child-parent relationships. And when parents significantly misrepresent God, they open the door to two major types of spiritual counterfeits. Both are ancient lies which are repackaged for each new generation, and both distort the truth about God's grace.

Counterfeit #1: No-Grace Theology

When it comes to God's grace—His unmerited favor toward sinful human creatures—many morally decent people say, in essence, "Thanks, but no thanks." The fatal flaw in no-grace theology is that, according to God Himself, "there is no one righteous . . . no one who does good, not even one" (Romans 3:10, 12). This doesn't mean that humans can't be nice and kind, even generous and compassionate. It's just that we can't be anything enough to earn our way into heaven.

In dealing with the Pharisees, the official good people of His day, Jesus said that only the sick need a doctor, not the healthy, and that He came to call sinners, not the righteous (Matthew 9:12–13). According to Jesus, no one is in perfect spiritual health. His point to the no-grace good guys was that as long as they refused to recognize and acknowledge their sin-sickness, they could not be healed because they would not come to Him, the Great Physician, for healing and salvation.

Some people adopt the no-grace counterfeit because they believe they are good enough *for* God. Others follow no-grace religions because they believe they are good enough *to be* God.

People with significant unseen wounds are at risk for modern versions of no-grace theology because it promises inner healing. Who doesn't want or need some kind of inner healing? Today's religious celebrities mix pop psychology and no-grace New Age spirituality in a nearly irresistible concoction that is being eaten up by many sincere seekers. Here, for example, is a description of a best-selling New Age book called *A Course in Miracles*.

The course consists of a text, a workbook, and manual with 365 lessons, one for each day. The faithful attend lectures and meditate. They also read from a Bible-like book, said to have been dictated by "a voice" to an admitted atheist psychologist named Helen Schucman over seven years in the mid-1960s. . . . *The purpose: inner healing.*

Ideas are based on universal spiritual themes, using Christian terms.[3]

Notice the phrase "using Christian terms." This traps many spiritually hungry seekers in deceptive and disastrous counterfeits of genuine biblical Christianity. And what is the central message of *A Course in Miracles* that's designed to bring inner healing? "The key to healing the human condition will come from our own hearts and minds."

If that sounds familiar, perhaps you're recalling the lie that Satan told Eve: "For God knows that when you eat from it . . . you will be like God" (Genesis 3:5). At the heart of New Age spirituality is the twisted teaching that neither God nor His grace is necessary for salvation.

Counterfeit #2: Some-Grace Theology

When our son, Dave, was young, he latched on to the phrase "busy as a beaver." Eventually, he shortened it to "beavering" and used it as a synonym for working frantically.

I've come to use the phrase "beavering for the Lord" to mean evangelical hyperactivity. Working for the Lord is fine as long as we're serving Christ from the overflow of loving, grace-filled hearts. It's not fine when we're beavering to pile up enough good deeds to outweigh the bad so we can earn a ticket to heaven or build a hedge against disaster.

Some-grace churches are filled with people beavering for the Lord. These busy churchgoers are descended from a long line of religious beavers, some of whom received one of the apostle Paul's sternest and most impassioned letters. We know it as the New Testament epistle to the Galatians.

Paul was astonished that the Christians in Galatia were deserting Christ and His grace (1:6), and he put his finger on their some-grace error. The Galatian believers began their faith lives relying totally on grace, but some fell away from believing in grace as the sole basis of being rightly related to God (5:4). Paul, in contrast, stated emphatically that he had not set aside grace nor replaced it with law keeping as his source of righteousness (2:21). In fact, he said that if righteousness could be obtained by keeping the law, then Jesus's death on the cross was a colossal error of cosmic proportions.

Some-grace theology implies that we begin our Christian lives depending one-hundred-percent on Christ's righteousness, but our dependence decreases as we develop more and more righteousness of our own through increasingly perfect law keeping. Some-grace churches—often those that are the loudest in proclaiming themselves to be Bible believing—beat the Galatians hands down with legalism.

Like the hurting and hurtful families they resemble, some-grace churches have expectations for their members that distort and deny the truth. As we've discussed, in hurtful families, expectations for children don't match the truth about child development and human imperfection. Likewise, in some-grace churches, the expectations for members don't match the biblical truth of spiritual growth and human imperfection. As a result, problem-laden believers often feel different and worth less than the mythical perfect Christians they're told they should be. And this leads to perfectionistic performances to earn the right to be with and relate to God and other supposedly perfect Christians. No wonder some-grace churches are like family reunions encased in stained glass. And no wonder the term "church home" brings chills, not thrills, to wounded worshipers.

The Some-Grace God

Some-grace churches frequently picture God as a frowning Pharisee and a stern shepherd. This god angrily drives his sheep to jump through higher and higher spiritual hoops to win his hard-to-earn acceptance. But no matter how hard we work, we can never satisfy this god. And when we fail? Well, let's just say it's not a pretty picture. He'll zap us with financial disasters and physical diseases to underscore his intolerance of our human imperfection and his impatience with our spiritual shortcomings.

> **Our salvation and right standing with God rest on Jesus's perfect performance, not ours.**

Hurting people can be deceived by this kind of spiritual counterfeit if they don't have the genuine article—a personal relationship with Jesus. But that requires trust, which isn't easy for those who have a distorted picture of God as heavenly Father.

Even though some-grace theology may be closer to the truth than no-grace theology, it still misses God's all-grace plan.

All-Grace Theology

In contrast to no-grace and some-grace counterfeits, Scripture declares that grace alone is the only foundation we can safely stand on. And we know we're standing on grace alone when the following formula summarizes our beliefs:

Jesus + Nothing Else = Acceptance by God

175

Our salvation and right standing with God rest on Jesus's perfect performance, not ours. If it were the other way around, whose praises would we sing throughout eternity? Why would we glorify and praise God the Father, Son, and Holy Spirit if we had done most of the work?

Churches and All-Grace Theology

Some churches seem to fear that if the truth about grace gets out—that God's gift of eternal life through Christ doesn't require any beavering—believers will abandon biblical guidelines for conduct and become a pack of howling hedonists. This view misses the truth that grace-awed believers *want* to obey and please God. We love Him as a natural response to His first loving us, not because we're trying to earn His favor.

What does your church believe about grace? Is it an all-grace group of love-led people learning to be real about themselves, their struggles, and their joys as they seek to make Jesus Lord of their lives? Or is it a fear-driven, cold collection of the frozen chosen living out wounded and weary some-grace legalism?

Church, as God intended it to be, is the place that when sinners go there, other sinners have to take them in—and none of us deserve it. That's what a genuinely Bible-believing church is and does.

The God of All Grace

Of all the challenges hurt people face, the most important is correcting their distorted concept of God. God is not just like our parents—even if they were good and godly. And He definitely is not like parents who were consistently hurtful.

Most break*throughs* require a "break *with*." This truth is well-known to wounded worshipers who long to see God more accurately. As Taylor, an incest survivor, put it, "I had to let go of my father's god before God could become my Father." That's no easy task for an incest survivor—or for any wounded worshiper. What Taylor and all of us need is some way to learn what our heavenly Father is truly like.

Knowing God: Provisions and Problems

The Bible provides the clearest picture of who God is. At the same time, the Bible presents a problem to wounded worshipers with "Bible phobia." In abusive churches, leaders often use Scripture as a weapon to keep members in line. So, Scripture for those Bible-beaten folks is often seen as an instrument of torture.

Kids who were punched in the nose every time they opened the refrigerator would learn to stay away from it and to survive on non-refrigerated food. However, when it comes to spiritual food, the Bible is our only source. Although creation reveals God's general existence, only the Bible gives specific revelation about God and His plan of redemption. Bible phobia is not a matter of failing to schedule time to read God's Word; it is being unable to read it without losing concentration, getting dizzy, or feeling ill. Anyone who has such a reaction needs help to work through spiritual abuse.

God knows that being in an intimate, loving relationship with Him is the source of our highest joy. He revealed Himself in Scripture so that we may know Him, trust Him, and love Him.

Trusting God: Problems and Purpose

The night before Jesus died, one of His disciples asked to be shown "the Father" (John 14:8). Jesus answered, "Anyone who has seen me has seen the Father" (v. 9). From Jesus's awesome answer flows healing for distorted God concepts. When we wonder how God wants to relate to us in various life circumstances, we need only look in Scripture and find out how Jesus did it.

God longs for us to know Him, and He put on skin so we could actually see Him. Jesus is "God with us" (Matthew 1:23). He's not just a discerning, departed teacher whose wise words are worth remembering. He is the visible, living, perfect God-man who knows and loves us and who calls us to know Him spiritually and personally so that we will trust Him. For hurting people, the thought of trusting anyone can be terrifying—and that includes God.

> When we wonder how God wants to relate to us in various life circumstances, we need only look in Scripture and find out how Jesus did it.

God offers Himself to us as a gift wrapped in flesh and named Jesus. But some who receive the gift become disappointed and disillusioned because it seems to be broken. Jesus doesn't work the way they were told He would. They thought life would be easy and exciting after receiving God's gift of salvation, and they hoped soon to be healthy, wealthy, wise, and hassle-free.

These unrealistic and unbiblical expectations about the Christian life are not the only problems we face when it comes to trusting God. Many of us can't seem to make it past our pain.

The Pain Barrier

The more wounded we were in childhood, the more difficult it is to trust God as adults. For Christians who grew up in substantially healthy homes, it's nearly impossible to fathom the depth of distrust felt by adult survivors of abuse.

God is much more realistic about all this than we are. For example, the Hebrew people enslaved in Egypt couldn't hear Moses's message from God because of their "discouragement and harsh labor" (Exodus 6:9). God wanted them to know that He had chosen them to be His people and that He would be their God in a special relationship that included release from bondage.

God understands the intense power of authentic emotions. After all, He created them. Somehow, we keep forgetting that. We need to see verses like this as God giving us permission to be as honest about the influence of authentic emotions in our lives as He is—even when those emotions include unspeakable terror that blocks our ability to trust.

> **Our parents, families, and friends may not give us permission to be fully human— feelings and all— but God does.**

Our parents, families, and friends may not give us permission to be fully human—feelings and all—but God does.

God isn't horrified when out of pain and despair we cry, "Why didn't you stop it? Why do you let it continue? Don't you care? What kind of Father are you?" If we risk being honest with ourselves and with God about our struggles to trust, we'll be in good company. King David and the other psalmists frequently addressed such questions to God. "O God, why have you rejected us forever?" (Psalm 74:1) is just one example. The prophet Habakkuk asked the same anguished question in these words: "Why are you silent while the wicked swallow up those more righteous than themselves?" (1:13).

God wants us to bring our fears, questions, and anguish to Him so we can experience His comforting embrace. He loves us, and He understands that until we know that He loves us, we will be unable to trust and love Him.

Loving and Relating to God

Oh, that we could get it straight once and for all: God loves us because of who *He* is, not because of who *we* are.

This all-grace good news of God's love and acceptance sounds too good to many of us—too good to be true, that is—especially to those of us weaned on phrases like "Anything worth having is worth working for." This gotta-work-for-it attitude sounds logical, but the more I learn about God, the more He stands my best logic on its head.

The relationship rules learned in hurting and hurtful families and the pathetic impersonations of perfection designed to guarantee acceptance all melt away in the warmth of God's unreasonable grace. But how hard it is to lay aside all our fancy footwork on the religious straight and narrow! I can only imagine what joy there will be in heaven when we finally collapse under the weight of our shame-fueled, fear-driven no-grace or some-grace religiosity. Only then will we fully experience God's love for us.

Jesus Loves (the Real) Me, This I (Finally) Know

My worst enemies could not be more surprised than I am at God's awesome, gracious love poured out on me, because I know more awful things about me than they do. And God knows far more than either they or I ever will. And here's the amazing part—God loves me anyway. As a Christian since age thirteen, I knew God loved me ("for the Bible tells me so") decades before I knew it in a deeply personal way. There is a world of difference between knowing about God's love theologically and knowing God's love experientially.

Specific Change Strategies

Some of us may need more help and healing before we can experience God's life-changing love. As always, we ground our change process in truth.

1. Begin thinking about God as Jesus. If you are serious about healing your spiritual abuse wounds, make an intentional choice to begin seeing Jesus whenever you think or talk about God. As I said earlier, the beginning of change is calling a thing by its right name. So, start by calling God "Jesus" rather than by the name of your father, stepfather, grandfather, or uncle.

Read and study the Gospels to learn how Jesus interacted with people. How did He treat people who were struggling with sin? I'll give you a hint. Jesus was astonishingly kind and gentle with people who knew they were sinful and amazingly confrontive with those who thought they were perfect.

2. Learn about God's general attributes. Learning to see God as He is revealed in Scripture—most clearly in Jesus, of course—will help you replace distorted God concepts with the truth. And this will help you love and trust God more. Appendix D lists some of God's attributes.

3. Learn about God as a loving parent. God wants us to know that He is not like hurtful human parents. Even though our parents forsake us, He "will take [us] up" (Psalm 27:10 NASB). That seems to picture God reaching down and adopting us as His own child, like a loving father would do for a child abandoned on his doorstep. In fact, Scripture repeatedly emphasizes God's tender concern for the fatherless and for orphans (see Psalms 10:14; 146:9; Hosea 14:3). Those verses have always been especially precious to me, a fatherless child.

4. Write about what you're learning. Journal about how God differs from the perception you have of Him that was shaped by your parents. How would this truth change your life if you began acting on it? One Christian adult raised by hurtful, perfectionistic parents made this observation:

> I am blown away by Jesus's description of the father in the parable of the prodigal son. He is entirely different from my dad. I have been afraid and very reluctant to confess my sins to God because I always pictured Him with His

arms folded over His chest, a disgusted look on His face, shaking His head back and forth—just like my dad. I think I can pray more easily if I can hold on to the picture of God as loving and forgiving.

5. *Get help to deal honestly with the pain of the pain.* When we begin to mourn our childhood losses and to feel the grief and despair, the pain can be debilitating. It can feel like dying. And the worst part may be the pain of the pain.

The pain of our pain is that God allowed it. I will not insult refugees from childhood hells by offering easy answers to the imponderable questions that such experiences raise. I don't know why our loving Father God permits children to undergo such unspeakable suffering. But I cling to my belief that somehow—in ways that are light-years beyond my capacity to understand—God will fulfill His promises to comfort the mourning and bring joy out of the pain (Psalm 30:11; Isaiah 61:2–3). If the pain of our pain is that God allowed it, then the joy of our joy must be learning that God can heal and redeem our pain and lead us into lives of genuine joy.

6. *Choose to trust God in the midst of your pain and questions.* If we insist on waiting until the pain and doubt go away before trusting God, we'll never do it. God never promised pain-free lives in this sin-stained world. But He has promised to be with us and to comfort and strengthen us in the midst of our pain. I invite you to examine His record of faithfulness to that promise and, after doing so, to purposefully decide to trust God. If you are willing to practice this choice (or even willing to be made willing), ask God to empower you.

7. *Choose your church family.* We couldn't choose our birth families, but we can choose our church families. Deliberately evaluate your church's spiritual health and decide whether you should stay. Make sure you are in a church that has the biblically

balanced emphasis of 2 Peter 3:18, which tells believers to "grow in grace and knowledge of our Lord and Savior Jesus Christ." Many churches put all their emphasis on the latter while neglecting the former—all the while calling themselves Bible-believing. It is possible to find churches that balance both; I know because I am in one. Ask God to lead you in this critical choice.

Healing for Worshipers' Wounds
Healing Overview and Progress Evaluation (HOPE) Chart

Key Issues	Seeing Truth	New Choices	New Practices
Learning to separate God's traits from our parents' traits	I've been relating to God as if He had the same expectations as my parents	Learn more about God's true character by learning more about Jesus	Relate consistently to God on the basis of His attributes as revealed in Jesus
Living by all-grace theology	Sometimes I live as if I don't need any grace or only some at the start of my faith life	Study the Bible to discover the role of God's grace in being rightly related to God	Relate consistently to God on an all-grace basis of trust in Jesus's righteousness and death for my sins
Choosing to trust God for comfort	I've trusted God to keep me pain-free or not trusted Him to comfort and guide	Learn from Scripture how faithful and trustworthy God has proven to be	Choose consistently to trust God for comfort in my pain and for guidance in my life

Pause to Ponder and Pray

Ponder

Use the HOPE chart to get an idea of where you are in your changing and healing process in the area of spiritual wounds.

- Read appendix D. What surprises you most about God's attributes as revealed in the Bible?
- Review the characteristics of some-grace churches and all-grace churches in appendix E. Which one does your church resemble?

Pray

> Lord, help me see you as the loving Father that your Word and your Son show you to be. And please teach me to trust you in the midst of my pain and doubt. Thanks for understanding how difficult all of this is for me. Amen.

CHAPTER THIRTEEN

HELP FOR HEALING FORGIVERS

How can God bear to know all the details of all the hurts of all the ages? I can hardly stand knowing a fraction of the facts about one situation. The situation I am thinking of involves a clergyman who molested nearly a hundred boys and girls over a period of years. Even worse, his superiors moved him from one parish to another to keep his crimes from becoming widely known. Dozens of men and women have testified publicly of their abuse at his hands.

I'm torn between weeping and raging over this one hideous example of treachery and betrayal. What can we do? Where do we go? How can we bear such life-shattering injustice and pain? How can we help those who must find a way to do so—the children who were betrayed, the parents who trusted the betrayers?

When I can't bear it—whatever it may be—I've learned that my best choice is to bare it to the Lord. *Bare* it, as in uncovering it, but also *bear* it in the sense of mentally carrying it to the nail-scarred feet of Jesus and leaving it there.

The Facts about Forgiving

Finding our way through the tangled underbrush of facts and fallacies about forgiveness can be quite an adventure.

The only trustworthy map is Scripture, and the best guide I've found is Joseph, the Old Testament hero who started his life as the pampered son of a wealthy man.

His older brothers weren't as fond of him as their father was, however, and out of their jealousy they sold their little brother as a slave to some traveling merchants. But with God's help and blessing, Joseph didn't remain in slavery. After thirteen long years, he rose to prominence in Egypt, becoming second in command to Pharaoh. When his brothers came to buy grain for their famine-stricken families, they didn't recognize Joseph. But he knew them. At last, Joseph had a chance to get even. But he passed up the opportunity.

Even after receiving much kindness from Joseph, his brothers could never quite believe that he had forgiven them. When their father died, they speculated that Joseph had waited until then to get his revenge, so they fell on their faces before him and offered to be his slaves.

The brothers' speech brought this reply from Joseph: "You intended to harm me, but God intended it for good to accomplish what is now being done, the saving of many lives" (Genesis 50:20). This verse illuminates two major facts about forgiving.

Fact #1: Forgiving Is Founded on Ruthless Realism

Joseph didn't beat around the bush. He told his brothers that he knew they intended to harm him. God never asks us to play around with truth or fake it for Jesus's sake. Never. Especially not in an area as important as forgiveness.

One of the clearest truths of forgiveness centers on God's role as sole dispenser of judgment. Joseph told his brothers that he would not usurp the role of God by punishing them for their sins against him (v. 19). That sounds fine for Joseph and his brothers, but when God's timetable doesn't match ours, it's not so fine.

Ever wonder why God is so slow to execute judgment on evildoers? According to the apostle Peter, God is patiently extending opportunities for them to turn to Him for salvation (2 Peter 3:15). What we label slowness is actually God's gracious patience at work.

Although Joseph did not take vengeance on those who wronged him, neither did he minimize the wrong done to him. Many of us tend to deny the full extent of the damage done to us by excusing, minimizing, or discounting the hurt, as though whatever happened—no matter how horrendous—couldn't have been all that bad since we survived. That was Brooke's perspective when she said, "This sounds pretty bad, doesn't it? But really, it's okay. It's not as bad as it sounds."

I heard variations of that statement every time Brooke began to talk about her neglect and abuse as a child. By minimizing the experience, Brooke protected herself from feeling the full pain of her self-absorbed parents' loveless parenting. With typical childlike magical thinking, Brooke concluded that she caused their behavior because she was, as she put it, "an unusually bad child." Brooke's perception that she was worth less than other people made her folks' actions seem "not as bad as it sounds."

After Brooke spent several sessions beginning to face the truth of her early life, I introduced a new question after one of her minimizing statements. Brooke was single and childless, so I asked her to think of our pastor's little girl who was the same age as Brooke during the period of abuse she had just recalled and then discounted. "Would that be okay if it had happened to the pastor's daughter?" I asked.

Brooke's face changed instantly. "Oh, dear God, no! Of course not. No," she exclaimed in horror.

"Then what made it okay for you?" I asked softly.

Shame tells us that whatever treatment we get is okay because, after all, it's just us.

Sometimes people think that such an attitude is humble and helpful to their process of change. But, as always, denial of truth impedes the healing we long to experience. We must forgive those who hurt us before we can live in the freedom God intends for us, but we must be ruthlessly realistic about what we are forgiving. That means we must name the deeds done to us, just as Joseph did, and stop deadening the emotions that accompany such deeds.

> We must forgive those who hurt us before we can live in the freedom God intends for us, but we must be ruthlessly realistic about what we are forgiving.

Ruthless realism also includes the recognition that those who hurt us very likely were hurt when they were children. Perhaps they were abandoned by neglect or terrorized by abuse. This reality, while helping us to understand the bad treatment we've received, in no way excuses it. We must be clear about this. Learning more about those who wounded us helps us forgive them without excusing or accepting their wrong choices.

Another ruthless reality is that refusing to forgive can make us feel as if we are in a position of power. It's as if we say, "I'll show them. They withheld so much from me for so long; I'll withhold forgiveness." One fallacy of this reasoning is that people who hurt others don't usually care about being forgiven. In fact, they may not even notice that forgiveness is being withheld. Refusing to forgive is like being a toddler who holds her breath because she's angry that her mother is ignoring her. But since the mother is ignoring the child, she doesn't notice, so the only one to suffer is the little girl who turns blue and gets dizzy.

The bottom line when it comes to ruthless realism is this: genuine forgiveness forces us to relinquish our fantasy of having a past that never was so we can see the truth of what is and what can be.

If the forgiving process sounds like a scary, messy business, you're listening well. But take heart. Joseph's experience reveals the secret to surviving the pain of genuine forgiving.

Fact #2: Forgiving Is for Those in God's Family

As God's child by faith, Joseph had access to his heavenly Father's provisions. We see this most clearly when Joseph credits God with enabling him to move beyond the pain of his past into a life of fruitfulness (Genesis 41:51–52).

We will never find the motivation or means to fully forgive—ourselves or others—unless we respond to the moving of God in our hearts the way Joseph did. After all, forgiving is an unnatural, illogical act. This is a dog-eat-dog world, not a dog-forgive-dog world. And people are more eager to demand an eye for an eye and a tooth for a tooth than to write off any wrongs done to them. Little wonder, then, that we bump and bruise each other as we stagger blind and toothless through our lives.

Forgiving is a family business. God wants His children to bear some likeness, however imperfectly, to Him, their heavenly Father. That's the message of verses like Ephesians 4:32, which tell us to be kind and forgiving like our Father God is.

But neither the promises of God nor the commands of God are universally applicable. Anyone who is trying to live by the Father's rules without being the Father's child needs to begin forgiving by receiving forgiveness.

> **Forgiving is a family business. God wants His children to bear some likeness, however imperfectly, to Him, their heavenly Father.**

Receiving Forgiveness for Ourselves

Unless we experience forgiveness, it is impossible to forgive others—especially when those others are parents who betrayed our tender trust during childhood.

The biblical basis for this me-first order of forgiving is found in Matthew 18:21–35. In answer to Peter's question about how much forgiving God expects from His children, Jesus told a story. The king in the story confronted one of his servants about repaying a multimillion-dollar debt. The servant asked the king to be patient and promised to repay everything. The king took pity on him, released him, and canceled the debt.

After the debt-free servant left, he found another servant who owed him a few dollars and demanded immediate payment. The second servant also asked for patience and promised to repay everything. But the first servant refused and had the poor guy thrown into prison.

When the king heard about this, he summoned the servant he had forgiven, denounced his lack of mercy, and turned him over to "the jailers to be tortured" (v. 34).

What can we learn from this story about the relationship between having our unpayable debts canceled and canceling the debts of others? Here are five principles.

1. Point: The first servant underestimated his debt and overestimated his ability to repay. That's why he asked for patience rather than mercy. *Principle*: We all underestimate the enormity of our sin debt and overestimate our ability to do enough good deeds to balance the scales.

2. Point: The king understood the truth about the debt and the debtor, so he gave the mercy that was needed instead of the time that was sought. *Principle*: God understands the depth of our sin and our spiritual bankruptcy even though we don't. Therefore, while we keep asking what we can do to earn eternal life, God keeps telling us that He canceled our sin debt through Jesus's death on the cross (Colossians 2:13–14).

3. Point: The debt-free servant did not really hear the king's incredibly gracious words; therefore, he believed that he still owed a debt he needed to pay eventually. *Principle*: This captures the essence of some-grace theology. The servant asked for some grace in the form of patience. But he figured he could do the rest on his own.

4. Point: That's why the first servant sought to collect a relatively small debt which his fellow servant actually might have been able to repay in time. *Principle*: Operating from a some-grace perspective means we don't have enough grace-consciousness to extend to others who owe us.

5. Point: The servant who refused to cancel a debt because he didn't believe his debt had been canceled experienced imprisonment and torture instead of the joy of living debt-free. *Principle*: People who see themselves as unreleased and debt-laden won't release others or cancel their debts. As a result, debt collectors live in torturous bondage.

Good News and Bad News about Being Forgiven

Our worst and God's best met on a battlefield called Calvary. God won! Jesus's victory there is God's good news to those who will receive it.

According to *The New International Dictionary of New Testament Theology*, *forgiveness* means "pardon" or "release from a debt."[1] Like the first servant in Jesus's story, we've been pardoned—released from our unpayable debt of sin. But like the debt-free servant, we must accept the gift and stop trying to pay the impossible debt ourselves.

Many of us still struggle to fully live each moment in the reality of God's amazing grace long after we have received His gift of forgiveness. Forgiveness is our theological certainty, but it has not become our experienced reality. Some Christians use self-punishing guilt in an attempt to make themselves behave better. The logic goes something like this: "I hate myself for what I did because I horribly hurt myself and others. I will continue to punish myself with guilt because it will keep me from sinning that way again." Believe me, this is bad news. Such reasoning keeps us so focused on what we have done that we all but ignore what Christ has done for us. Without a shift of focus from our sins to God's grace, we'll never experience the freedom forgiveness brings. And only the forgiven can truly forgive.

Forgiving Our Parents

"It isn't just what they did. It's who did it!"

That's how Tim described what hurt him most about growing up with a verbally abusive mother and a physically abusive father.

Parents are supposed to nurture and protect their children, but not all of them do. And children who come from hurtful families have more to forgive than ordinary childhood wounds.

I've told you enough about my mother-focused childhood for you to realize that I remained overly invested in my mother's life well into my adult years. So you can imagine how shocked I was many years ago when she phoned me and matter-of-factly announced that she'd been married for six weeks to a man I'd never even heard her mention. I maintained my cheery sunshine voice throughout our conversation and did not begin to let myself feel the tangled mix of emotions until weeks later.

I felt so abandoned and betrayed. Over and over I said to myself, "I would never have done that to her!" And it was true. I would never even have considered such a thing. I began to feel an indescribable sense of having been suckered by my mother into working hard, jumping through hoops, and twisting myself into a human pretzel my entire life trying to make her happy because she counted on me so much. But how important was I actually? She didn't even bother telling me about her wedding until six weeks after the fact, not to mention failing to invite me to attend or participate. Her wedding, for goodness' sake!

That was one of my earliest clues to just how deeply wounded and self-absorbed my mother was.

I realize that this experience pales in comparison to many examples of how wounding parents continue their hurtful ways even after their children are adults. Unless hurtful parents—and the others who hurt us—open themselves to the healing touch of God, they will go on wounding us as long as we or they are alive.

We need to do something with the growing mountains of hurt that threaten to crush us with hatred and bitterness. Releasing the hurts and the hurters from their debt to us is our only hope. And if we can release our parents, the rest of the wounding world is a cinch.

Releasing Our Hurtful Parents

What we hold holds us. It's true of our belief systems. It's also true of unforgiveness.

I've been told that a monkey is trapped when it slips its hand into a tiny opening in a cage to grab something desirable like a banana. The monkey's banana-clutching fist is too large to get back through the opening, so it stays trapped unless the monkey releases what it's holding. Apparently monkeys seldom are willing to do that.

How about you? Pause a moment and pick up something small that won't break (like a piece of paper). Now open your hand, palm down, and notice what happens. As you release what you've been holding, it releases you. Now your hand is free to reach for anything you want.

"But it seems so unfair for me to be hurt over and over without somebody admitting guilt or paying for it," some argue in response to the suggestion of releasing their hurters.

Some think they could forgive and release if only the wounders would say they were sorry. But even if they did, the level of repentance might not match the level of wounding.

In a television special about child abuse, the host talked with a convicted incest perpetrator and one of the two stepdaughters he sexually abused for nearly a decade. Although he had served nine years in prison for his crime, he was still reluctant to own his sin against his stepdaughters. Even when he finally did, it was more like a half admission—squeezed out of him by the host who repeatedly confronted his failure to accept full responsibility.

The man's "If I hurt you, I'm sorry" pseudo repentance fell far short of his level of wounding.

Ask yourself this: What could hurters possibly do today to make up for what they did yesterday? The answer? Nothing. They owe debts they can never repay.

Our hurters stand before us with empty hands and pockets, utterly unable to pay for the past. And we stand before them with two choices. One, we can keep trying to collect the debts they rightfully owe by exacting verbal and nonverbal tolls. But to do so, we also have to keep their deficits on our mental balance sheets, and this means we must constantly remind ourselves of the painful past. Two, we can cancel their debts and forgive them.

> **Forgiveness is not letting someone get away with sin; it's letting Jesus be the judge of it.**

Remember, forgiving is not denying the wrong they did; it's releasing the right to wrong them in return. Does that mean they get away with it? No. No one ever gets away with sin. Forgiveness is not letting someone get away with sin; it's letting Jesus be the judge of it. Forgiving means placing the sins and the sinners into the nail-scarred hands of the only One qualified to judge. In doing so, we are released from the bondage of bitterness that comes after our repeated attempts to exact justice have failed.

Not only is Jesus the way, the truth, and the life; He's also the door through which we must go to exit the trap of bitterness.

Self-wounding fantasies say, "I'm better off holding on to this bitterness and hatred." But if that's such an effective strategy, why are so many still in so much pain? Maybe unforgiveness hurts us even more than it hurts those who hurt us.

In "The Gift of Forgiveness," Arnold Fox and Barry Fox write: "Forgiveness allows your body to turn down the manufacture of those chemicals which are tearing you apart, body and soul. Doctors can give you all sorts of medicines for your headaches, your heart, your stomach pains, your spastic colon, your anxiety and other problems. But the medicines will not get to the root of the problem: 'Unforgiveness.' The cure for that lies in forgiving. When you savor your hatred, you don't hurt 'them,' you hurt 'yourself.'"[2]

Resentment and bitterness are malevolent forms of interpersonal attachment—like being tied with barbed wire to people who hurt us. How much longer before we realize that we, not they, are the ones most bloodied? Here is a poem I wrote while pondering this idea:

> "Release the prisoner! Release or he will die."
> "Release the prisoner? Where's justice?" my
> reply.
> "Release the prisoner!" I heard again the cry.
> Release the prisoner? At last, I said I'd try.
> Release the prisoner, with Grace my sole
> supply,
> I released the prisoner and saw that it was I.

Releasing those who have hurt us includes recognizing the ruthless reality that they are as bankrupt before us as we are before God.

When we finally snip our barbed-wire bitterness and release ourselves from them, we can move on to consider an even more outrageously unreasonable proposal.

195

Choosing Our Parents

"Choose my parents? You've got to be kidding!" That was my response when I heard a wise people helper say that all of us must come to the place of choosing our parents. In so doing, the person said, we choose God and, in fact, we choose ourselves.

I knew I had heard something as profound as it was unsettling, but I wasn't yet ready to wrestle with it. So I locked it tightly in my emotion-proof cognitive box until a more convenient time, which I assumed would not be for months, maybe even years.

A few days later, during a time of Bible study and prayer, the Holy Spirit shattered my intellectualization, and I began to see a long line of smiling young mothers walking past a hospital nursery window, looking in at me in my bassinet. When I saw my own mother, I reached up and sensed myself being lifted into her waiting arms. I could feel my tiny infant body resting on her shoulder, enfolded by her arms.

I sobbed and sobbed, clutching a sofa pillow to my chest and abdomen as if to keep my emotional guts from exploding through my skin. Between sobs, I began to repeat aloud, "Yes, Mother, I choose you because God chose you for me." (Tears come to my eyes even as I write this.) I also told my mother, in my heart, that I remembered many painful circumstances, but I was still choosing her. I thanked her for loving me, for fighting to give me life, and especially for teaching me about God's love.

I was completely exhausted when I finished, and I felt as if I'd lost fifty pounds—right over my heart. I have meaningful and precious times of prayer and Bible study regularly, but that sort of experience is definitely not business as usual.

You may be appalled by the thought of choosing your parents, just as I was at first. But think of it this way: until we emotionally accept, receive, and, yes, choose our parents, we are rejecting the instrument of our birth and our genetic endowment. This symbolic, emotional choice in no way negates the reality of our parents' behavior toward us. Remember, God never asks us to choose denial of pain and terrible truth. God asks us to choose to trust Him to heal the pain and transform the truth.

Forgiveness, Boundaries, and Reconciliation

One reason for recoiling at the notion of emotionally choosing our parents may be the mistaken belief that we are forfeiting the right to establish any personal boundaries with them. In reality, neither releasing our parents to God nor receiving our parents from God requires us to relinquish healthy interpersonal boundaries. Why? Because grace is free; trust is earned.

> **Grace is free; trust is earned.**

This crucial distinction means that we can forgive and release people from their debts to us without giving them unlimited access to our lives. Boundaries mark levels of trust. If you embezzle funds from my company, I can forgive you without asking you to be my accountant.

But what about reconciliation? Don't we have to fully reconcile when we fully forgive? I don't think so. Forgiveness can be accomplished by one party; reconciliation requires two. Reconciliation is rooted in both parties agreeing about the truth of the wrongdoing (see 2 Corinthians 5:18–21). Where there is no agreement, there can be forgiveness but no reconciliation. When a hurt person moves to extend forgiveness and seek reconciliation and is called crazy, a liar, or a dozen other things, none of which agree with the truth, reconciliation cannot take place.

God speaks so much about forgiveness for two main reasons. First, we have only other sinners to relate with, so we need to become skillful forgivers. Second, God makes forgiveness a centerpiece of our healing process because living in unforgiveness is so much worse.

Specific Change Strategies

1. Receive God's forgiveness. People who feel unforgiven are poor forgivers. Turn back to the prayer at the end of chapter 7. With those or similar words, commit yourself to God and receive His forgiveness through Christ. Then you can begin focusing on God's grace instead of your sins.

2. Learn more about forgiveness. Scripture is the best source of information, so consider doing a Bible study on the topic of forgiveness.

3. Adopt and structure an "event and process" perspective on forgiving. A good analogy comes from the years my husband and I lived on a tiny lake. Sailing from our dock to the end of the lake began with an event that included a decision to reach that goal. Yet it also required a process of continually recommitting to that goal as gusts of wind and our own wandering attention got us off course.

Use something like the following Declaration of Forgiveness to structure your formal forgiving event. It can help you head back toward your forgiveness goal when gusts of new memories arise and emotional storms blow you temporarily off course.

Sharing your decision to forgive reinforces the reality of that choice. The witness who signs your declaration could be a trusted friend, a Christian counselor, a pastor, or someone else who understands your pain and the significance of your forgiving.

Declaration of Forgiveness

To:

Date:

This is what you chose to do that hurt me:

This is how your hurtful choice has continued to hurt me as an adult:

I recognize that because God has forgiven me, He directs and empowers me to forgive you, whether or not my feelings match my volitional choice.

Therefore, I, _____,
hereby release _____ from the debt owed me because of his/her hurtful choice(s).

I will continue to reaffirm my choice to forgive, understanding that new memories and emotional storms may temporarily blow me off course. (God knows and I know that I am not perfect at forgiving any more than at anything else.) I will continue to meditate upon God's grace and forgiveness toward me.

Signature _____

Witness _____

4. Relabel those you've forgiven. This is especially meaningful in forgiving parents. For example, we might relabel "guilty mother" as "mother released to God."

5. Get help to process the intense and painful emotions that accompany forgiveness. My admittedly simple forgiveness formula is this: face it, feel it, and forgive it. The second step can be a killer. Don't attempt a Lone Ranger imitation—especially when it comes to working through the pain of forgiving.

6. Consider confronting the people you have forgiven. Sounds contradictory, doesn't it? But think of it this way: when we give offenders a chance to admit their wrongdoing against us, we are being more merciful and loving than if we let them continue unchallenged and unrepentant until they are confronted by

God. Also, if we know that they are still hurting others as they hurt us, God calls us to expose their "deeds of darkness" (Ephesians 5:11). If these dark deeds include sexual or physical child abuse, we may need to do more than just confront the abusers.

Child abuse is not only a sin; it's also a crime. If child abusers are unwilling to stop their criminal sinning and get help, we need to report them to authorities who will see that they do. Please note: We can forgive criminal sins yet still report and prosecute the sinner. Many victims, especially if they and their abusers are Christians, get confusing and unbiblical counsel on this. These dear people may be told that 1 Corinthians 6:1–8 forbids Christians to report and prosecute other Christians. In fact, this reasoning has been used repeatedly to allow church-going offenders to continue for years in their sins.

The truth is that 1 Corinthians 6 refers to civil cases—like fights over a piece of property—not criminal cases. Romans 13:1–6 describes God's provision for dealing with criminal acts.

Some counselors say that we can never truly forgive without confronting. False. This is like saying we must fully reconcile to fully forgive. What if our hurters are dead? We can neither reconcile with nor confront them. And even when they are alive, they can short-circuit reconciliation with lies.

When we choose to confront, we need practical and prayer-filled preparation. In truth, this holds for every step in the excruciating and crucial journey called forgiveness.

Healing for Forgivers' Wounds
Healing Overview and Progress Evaluation (HOPE) Chart

Key Issues	Seeing Truth	New Choices	New Practices
Understanding what genuine forgiveness is and is not	I don't understand what genuine biblical forgiving is	Learn about what genuine forgiving is and is not	Consistently practice genuine biblical forgiving

Key Issues	Seeing Truth	New Choices	New Practices
Experiencing the reality of God's forgiveness	I have not accepted the gift of God's forgiveness in Christ	Ask for and receive God's forgiveness by accepting Christ's payment for my sin debt	Living more often in the freedom and joy of knowing my entire sin debt is paid
Releasing my hurters into God's hands	I have refused to forgive and release those who've hurt me	Consider the benefits of forgiving and releasing those who've hurt me	Actually forgive and emotionally release my hurters to God

Pause to Ponder and Pray

Ponder

Use the HOPE chart to get an idea of where you are in your changing and healing process in the area of forgiveness.

- Were you surprised by what forgiveness is and is not? Why or why not?
- Where are you in the three-step forgiveness formula? Have you faced your wounds? Felt your emotions? Forgiven those who have wounded you?
- If you're stuck, unable to move to the next step, will you get some help? If so, when?

Pray

*Lord, thank you for paying my debt of sin
since I never could. Please empower and
comfort me as I face the truth and feel the
pain of my hurts, so that I can forgive
others as you've forgiven me. Amen.*

CHAPTER FOURTEEN

HELP FOR
HEALING PARENTS

Anything that begins with the word *labor* can't be easy. This is certainly true of parenting.

Many parents who grew up in hurtful homes use the "muddle-through model" of parenting with their own children. This leaves them feeling as if they're performing brain surgery at midnight in a dark room with one hand tied behind them. They suspect that there's a lot more they need to know, but they don't know what they don't know.

Most parents, when scratched, hemorrhage guilt and shame. As one member of a support group for adult children of dysfunctional families put it, "My greatest fear is that twenty or thirty years from now, my kids will be coming to this group."

We have a lot more influence than many of us *want* to have with our children. I think of this whenever I hear parents say, "But I didn't mean to hurt my kids." That's true in the vast majority of situations involving hurtful parents.

What traps parents into repeating the painful patterns of their own parents is the unwillingness to accept that each of us is imperfect and so is our knowledge. Once again we see the hurtful legacy of unbiblical, binding shame.

Imagine that the world of interpersonal relationships is a

ballroom, and I have two broken legs. Because I believe that broken legs are unforgivable moral flaws, I refuse to acknowledge the pain from my leg problem. What's more, I insist on dancing every number, no matter how fast the tempo, while pretending that my legs are fine. Consequently, I refuse all offers of assistance while I stumble here, stagger there, and leave a trail of crushed toes and bruised ankles in my zigzagging wake.

That strange scene is a picture of parenting patterns when we keep operating from shame-shaped thinking that believes every problem is a moral flaw. All of us, to some extent, are hurt people, so we all have broken legs, so to speak. The more shame-bound we are, the more we'll deny that reality and refuse life-changing assistance.

And who's most likely to get clobbered in our zigzagging? Those closest to us, including our children, who end up with bruised legs of their own. They will then develop self-protective (and problematic) patterns, which, if continued, will pull their offspring into this painful intergenerational dance. And on and on it goes.

Now picture that imaginary ballroom as very dimly lit. Slowly the lights come up, and we begin to recognize the extent of our wounding ways on those nearest and dearest to us. From one corner of the relational ballroom to the other, people are moaning.

"But I was dancing the best I could," we lament. "I didn't mean to crush your toes, bruise your ankles, or break your legs."

When parents begin to recognize the extent of their wounds and their wounding ways, some become so overwhelmed that they focus all of their attention on their children to help them heal. In our concern for our children, however, we often lose sight of a truth we hear proclaimed each time we board a commercial airplane.

Secure Your Own Oxygen Mask First

If you're like me, you don't listen very attentively to safety speeches. But every time a flight crew prepares for takeoff, one of the attendants recites a parable that illustrates a major struggle of parents raised in unhealthy homes. After pointing out the emergency exits and explaining the flotation cushions, the flight attendant says, "In case of a decrease in cabin pressure, oxygen masks will be released. If you are traveling with small children, secure your own oxygen mask first and then that of your child."

The instructions about oxygen masks convey an indispensable parenting truth: Unless we first help ourselves, we won't be able to help our children. Unless we choose life-giving truth, we won't be able to lead our children into truth-filled living. To many, this me-first approach seems inexcusably selfish, especially for those genuinely concerned for their children.

> **Unless we first help ourselves, we won't be able to help our children.**

It's as if, clutching our throats and nearly unconscious, we gasp, "I can't be bothered worrying about my breathing. Just tell me how to help my children breathe better."

When my children were ages seven and nine, I parented in the Twilight Zone for about six months. Clinical depression turned me into a virtual zombie. I was living proof that Job 14:21–22 is true:

> If their children are honored, they do not
> know it;
> if their offspring are brought low, they do
> not see it.
> They feel but the pain of their own bodies
> and mourn only for themselves.

My personal pain was blocking my awareness of my children's ups and downs. Things got so bad that our family physician referred me to a psychiatrist. I was sleeping about eighteen hours most days, and the doctor said I was irreparably damaging my body.

With the characteristic self-loathing of someone experiencing depression, I did not consider myself, or my emotional condition, important enough to warrant paying a psychiatrist's fee. But I finally went, took the prescribed medication I despised, and began the painful process of healing unseen wounds. But I did it for only one reason: I did not want to continue sleeping away Becky's and Dave's childhoods.

Depression depleted my capacity to care about myself and nearly everything else in life, but it didn't destroy my love for my children. But loving my children wasn't enough to help either them or me. I had to let that love motivate me to reach, as it were, for my own oxygen mask. *I was forced to become a healthier person so I could become a healthier parent!*

In our concern for our children, we have to remember to keep reaching for our own oxygen masks of truth-based healing and change. That's how we become increasingly healthy parents, better able to help our children change.

One of the most challenging aspects of this changing, as it applies to our parenting roles, is learning to sift what we learned from our parents and separate the lies from the truth.

Major Challenge #1: Separating Parenting Lies and Truths

The following chart will help you start this sifting process.[1]

Comparing Parenting Lies and Truths

Lies	Truths
Parents are giant geniuses who will always be smarter and stronger than their children.	Parents are older human beings, so they have more information and physical strength than children. Under normal circumstances, children will be about as smart (or smarter) and as strong (or stronger) someday.

Lies	Truths
Children are selfish and cause trouble when they have personal needs that inconvenience their parents.	All children have legitimate personal needs that often inconvenience their parents. This is one of the realities of parenting.
All parents are supposed to protect and direct their children forever since parents will always know more than their children.	Parents are supposed to protect and direct their children while they are young. As children get older, parents are supposed to teach them how to protect themselves in most situations and how to seek God's protection and direction in all situations.
Parents are supposed to love their children more when they obey them and make them look good.	Children should not have to earn their parents' love. Parents are supposed to love their children unconditionally.
Children are supposed to make their parents happy.	Children do not have the power to make their parents, or anybody else, happy any more than anyone else has the power to make them happy.
Children are supposed to please their parents, and if they work hard enough and are good enough, they will be able to please their parents.	Being pleased is a function of someone's personal value system. People are supposed to live to please God. This may or may not please their parents too.
Children are supposed to meet all their parents' needs and give them a reason to feel good about themselves; that is, children should fix their parents.	Children do not have the power to fix their parents or any other person. God doesn't send children to fix parents. He sent Jesus to do that.

Which side of the chart sounds more like the family you grew up in? If it's the side labeled "Lies," you likely grew up in a shame-bound family that had a negative effect on your own parenting patterns.

Byron is a committed Christian, respected counselor, and dedicated husband and dad. Byron also is the only offspring from the miserable union of an alcoholic father and a controlling mother. Byron's dad died years ago, and his mom lives several states away from her son and his family. Every year, Byron packs up his family and treks to his mom's place. One year, his sons, ages eight and ten, noticed how agitated Byron became the closer they got to Grandma's house. Byron explained that it was not a very relaxed and pleasant time for him because he had lots of sad memories about what happened in that house when he was about their age.

The older boy asked for some examples, and Byron carefully worded his response as he described his mother's attempts to control his thoughts and actions. When he finished, his ten-year-old son replied, "So, let me get this straight. When you were a kid, your mother was your brain."

If our parents insisted on being our brains, we're likely to live and parent on the "Lies" side of the chart. When we mistake being parent-brained for being loyal, we will fail to examine the patterns modeled for us by our parents. But when we clutch the same unexamined views at forty that we held at twenty, we're not uncompromising; we're just unteachable.

We will remain unteachable until we give ourselves permission to develop our own brains by sifting our beliefs about parent-child relationships and separating the wheat from the chaff. You'll notice I did not say we should assume that everything we learned from our parents is a pack of lies. I know parents who operate by this parenting method. One of them summarized it this way: "I ask myself what my folks would do in this situation, and then I do the exact opposite."

In contrast to this all-or-nothing thinking, our heavenly Parent tells us to examine all things carefully and to hold on to only what is genuinely good, right, and true (see 1 Thessalonians 5:21). Let yourself begin to experience the freedom inherent in this divine directive. It means you and I can use our God-given brains and move into the healthier, more biblical concepts of parent-child relationships as expressed on the right side of the chart above. If we reclaim our brains and make that mental shift, we are ready to take on the second major parenting challenge.

Major Challenge #2: Shifting Parenting Loyalties

Do you put more thought and emotional energy into being your parents' child or into being your child's parent? An honest answer to this question can change our lives as well as our parenting practices. How I wish someone had asked me this before we had our children. Since no one did, I had to stumble into this loyalty-shift business on my own. And I bruised my kids as I stumbled.

I was raised believing that one law of the universe was that good mothers have daughters who play the piano. As a parent, I knew my mother felt better when she saw me mothering the way she did. So, naturally, I determined to please my mother by squeezing my daughter into a musical mold.

> Do you put more thought and emotional energy into being your parents' child or into being your child's parent?

Becky is a person of many talents and interests, but she wasn't thrilled with my push to make her pour all her energy into a Steinway. In fact, the more I pushed, the more Becky hated the piano. And I was totally clueless as to why I had such a relentless compulsion to keep pushing. I simply and sincerely believed that I was doing what every good mother should do.

I'm not sure what happened. Maybe I finally heard Becky when she said, for the zillionth time, "Just because you loved to play the piano doesn't mean I have to. I'm not you." (She understood more about individuality at eight than I did at thirty-three.) After Becky left for school that morning, I prayed and wept before the Lord about the entire situation.

God reminded me of all the times my mother had conveyed that my piano recitals, radio programs, and other musical activities were more about her being a good mother than they were about me using my God-given ability. I saw too that I had believed Becky's musical performance was a commentary about me and my parenting abilities rather than a commentary about her and her musical abilities.

As long as I held a perspective that children exist to validate their parents, I had to make Becky keep taking piano lessons so that the world would know I was a good mother. It sounds very melodramatic now, but that morning I took a momentous step in my life and my parenting. Perhaps for the first time, I understood the need to transfer my primary loyalty from being my parent's child to being my child's parent.[2]

My loyalty shift meant that I let Becky stop taking piano lessons. On a broader scale, I reordered my skewed priorities and began appreciating Becky for the uniquely precious person she is.

Do you recognize what I was doing before my purposeful loyalty shift? By making my daughter perform to earn my acceptance, I was weakening my relationship with her so I could strengthen my relationship with my mother, who made me perform to earn her acceptance. Even after all these years, it still hurts to see that and say that. I used my daughter to gain my mother's approval. We all do that, to one degree or another, until we make the essential mental shift from child-of-my-parent to parent-of-my-child.

Changing Patterns of Performance-Based Self-Worth

When we believe the lie that says only perfect people deserve life and love, we are likely to experience existence guilt. When this is the case, we may unknowingly use our children as resources to validate our worthiness by expecting them to look perfect so we will look perfect. This replicates the core wounding mechanism our parents used with us.

We see this in the approaches we use to motivate our children. Shame-based child motivation reflects our attitudes about ourselves, which of course we learned from our parents. What does this kind of parenting look like? The following chart can help you recognize whether you view yourself and your children from a shame-based and performance-focused perspective.[3]

Contrasting Self and Child Motivation Approaches

Helpful Attitudes and Actions *See Self and Child as Human Beings*	Hurtful Attitudes and Actions *See Self and Child as Human Doings*
I belong to God by creation (and if I have asked Jesus to be my Savior and Lord, by salvation), so my major task is to know and love God and seek to do His will for my life.	I belong to my parents and to others who need and care for me. My major task is to please and perform for them (as perfectly as possible) so they will approve of me so I can feel good about myself.
My child belongs to God, so my major task is to help my child be the person God created my child to be by teaching him or her to know and trust God.	My child belongs to me, so I have the right to press my child into the service of my shame-based perfectionistic needs.
I emphasize the internal perspective of developing my own and my child's character.	I emphasize an external perspective of promoting and polishing my own and my child's performance.
I take a long view for the purpose of character development; for example, I let my child learn the consequences of procrastination by getting a poor grade on a project done the night before it's due.	I take a short view for the appearance of perfect performance; for example, I do my child's project myself the night before it is due so that my child will maintain the highest possible grades.

Helpful Attitudes and Actions *See Self and Child as Human Beings*	Hurtful Attitudes and Actions *See Self and Child as Human Doings*
I talk primarily about my child as an authentically struggling Christian, a very loving spouse, a tenderhearted boy or girl, a sincerely questioning teen, an honest employee, a wise parent, or a lover and student of God's Word.	I talk primarily about my child as the doctor, the ballet star, the select soccer hero, the youngest company vice president in history, the pee-wee league all-star, or the winner of the Sunday school's Bible verse memorization contest.
I usually ask myself and my child, "Did you enjoy yourself or learn anything?"	I usually ask myself and my child, "Did you win?" or "Were you the best?"
In myself and in my child, I affirm and reward brave attempts as well as obvious successes.	In myself and in my child, I affirm and reward winning only and believe that second place is no place.

Which style seems more familiar? Remember, we tend to parent the way we were parented, which is just what our parents did. So don't shame yourself for not knowing how to be a consistently adequate and non-shaming parent. We can learn what we don't know, but we can't learn what we refuse to admit that we don't know.

Kids or Crowbars?

Some of us have spent our lives trying to unlock the door to our parents' hearts. Without realizing it, we started using our kids as crowbars to pry open the storehouse of parental approval, which so far had been rationed in tiny bits or denied all together.

If we fail to shift our focus from being a child to being a parent, we'll continue using our kids as crowbars.

The kids-as-crowbars mentality springs directly from shame. Here's the logic: "If I had been a better child, my parents would have been better parents. They didn't love or approve of me because I wasn't as good as other children. But my children are good and lovable enough to earn my parents' approval. If I keep urging my kids to do everything my parents wanted me to do—and do it perfectly—maybe someday my parents will approve of me too."

Despite our best efforts (and our obsessive attempts to use our children's best efforts), few of us will receive the sought-after emotional nurture for one simple reason: our parents have none to give. The inheritance we want to receive from them was stolen years ago by trust bandits.

Clearly, most parents are not completely empty. But if your parents were extremely hurting and hurtful, assume that they are empty and ask yourself this painful question: "If my parents were ever going to give me loving acceptance and approval, wouldn't they have done it by now, considering how hard I've worked for it?"

> It's time to begin accepting your parents as they are—as they *really* are.

No matter how old you are, or how much energy you think you have to devote to the pursuit of parental love, it's time to begin accepting your parents as they are—as they *really* are. Only when we give up the dream of perfectly loving and nurturing parents can we stop wasting energy trying to get from our parents what they are unable to give. And only then can we use that energy to alter the course of our family's future. And that's no small achievement.

Cycle Breakers and Cycle Makers

All of us must answer this question: Will we continue to run the assigned laps in a wretched relay of intergenerational pain—that ongoing cycle of hurting, hating, and hurting again? Or will we stop running, break the cycle, and start a new cycle of healing and helping?

"I just wish I could start over with what I know now. I'd be a much better dad if I could just start over again." That's how Jeremy expressed his frustration about not beginning his changing, healing process until his three children were young adults. I told Jeremy what I'm telling you and myself: we can start over again—and again and again.

We can't go back to the first step of parenting, but we can start over where we are. We can't change what's gone before us, and we certainly can't change our parents. But we can change what comes after us because we can change our children's parents. Our heavenly Parent is deeply committed to this parent-child issue. He intends that the hearts of parents and children be turned toward each other (Malachi 4:6).

If you have repeatedly and recklessly wounded your children, God may be the only parent who can reach them. Their hearts may be turned away from and shut tight against you. If they will listen, ask your children to forgive you, but be prepared for disinterest, anger, or any number of responses other than forgiveness. If you cannot contact your children, begin praying that God will open the hearts that are closed to you.

Finally, how do we cope with the pain of realizing that we've hurt our children? We entrust them to the father heart of God, who loves them more than we do and who wants all of us to learn that only He can comfort and heal us from our hurt.

Specific Change Strategies

1. Learn as much as possible about healthy, biblical parenting. Read good books, attend parenting seminars, and find some consistently adequate parents who model the principles you are learning.

2. Tell your children that you intend to change your parenting practices. In an age-appropriate manner, let them know that you will be practicing new, healthier ways of relating to them. Tell them, however, that you won't ever be a perfect parent any more than they will be perfect children.

3. Get help to stop using your children to win approval from or to keep peace with your parents. Most of us have trouble seeing when we're doing this; that's why we need help. This is essential for those who were physically or sexually abused by a relative or family friend. Without realizing it, we may expose our children to dangerous situations with unsafe family members unless we experience healing.

4. Lovingly launch your children on their own healing, changing journeys. We can transform a hurtful heritage into a life-giving legacy. This is how Sarah did it.

Sarah came from a religious but abusive home. When she came to me for counseling, she had a deep love for Christ, a seminary degree, and a broken heart. The longer we worked together, the more she realized how deeply she had wounded her three children with her violent, angry outbursts.

As her personal healing progressed, she wanted to give her children something she had never received from her own parents—permission to get help for healing. At my suggestion, she wrote the following letter, which she planned to give to her three children when they were older.

> My precious children,
>
> I want you to know that I have deep regrets and anguish for having been a dysfunctional parent to you. I have betrayed your innocence and the trust you had in me numerous times over the course of your young lives. Though I have apologized to you and have expressed my remorse, I know extensive damage and brokenness have occurred within your emotions and spirits.
>
> Tears well up in my eyes when, in your sweet innocence, you tell me you love me. And you are just that—totally innocent. Nothing you did and nothing about you deserved the wounds you received from me. I am ashamed that I

have caused you these horrible hurts and scars. My heart agonizes over the thoughts of the emotional surgeries you will go through to recover from the emotional damage.

As the injuries are opened and examined, you will have times when you feel only anger and rage at me. It will not be easy for you to face such ugliness. But I want you to receive wise and skilled counsel; I want you to feel free to tell the truth—the horrible, painful truth. You don't need to protect me. Your healing and recovery are more important. I know you will never be able to fully forgive me, or fully get past these hurts, until you have thoroughly seen what it is you need to forgive and what needs to be healed.

I really do love you,
Mom

This is an example of how a parent's new, healthy choice to get help frees children to get help. This woman was determined, with God's guidance and empowering, to break the intergenerational cycle of abuse in her family.

Many of us would give almost anything to receive a letter like this from a parent, but few of us ever will. However, even if we never have a parent like this, by God's grace and our commitments to change, we can become a parent like this.

Healing for Parents' Wounds
Healing Overview and Progress Evaluation (HOPE) Chart

Key Issues	Seeing Truth	New Choices	New Practices
Separating parenting lies from truths	I've not ever purposefully evaluated my parenting beliefs	Separate the truth from the lies in my parenting beliefs	Consistently think and act on truth in my role as a parent

Key Issues	Seeing Truth	New Choices	New Practices
Shifting primary parenting loyalty	I've been focused more on being my parents' child than on being my child's parent	Put more thought and energy into being my child's parent and less into being my parents' child	Consistently choose to be more invested in the role of my child's parent than in the role of my parents' child

Pause to Ponder and Pray

Ponder

Use the HOPE chart to get an idea of where you are in your changing and healing process in the area of parenting wounds.

- Compare the lies and truths about parent-child relationships on pages 205–6. Where is your greatest struggle?
- How does your struggle manifest in your relationships with your children?
- What do you need to do to improve those relationships?
- Are you willing to do that? When will you begin?

Pray

Lord, I confess that I often value my children most for what they do to make me look good. Please help me to love and accept them for who they are—precious bearers of your image and priceless gifts from your hand. Amen.

CHAPTER FIFTEEN

HELP FOR HOPEFUL TOMORROWS

The healing process is like trying to package a live octopus. Just about the time we think it's all wrapped up, something else pops out. That's why it's more realistic to say "I'm committed to a changing process" rather than "I'm completely changed."

As shown throughout this book, change means choosing a new direction. But some of us still wrestle with the idea that change is a journey, not a destination, and that the journey proceeds one step at a time, as twelve-step programs say.

Sometimes our steps are buoyant, bounding leaps. Other times they are more like lead-footed shuffling or about-to-crash stumbling. Usually they're something in between. But as long as we're shuffling or stumbling in a new, healthier, more truthful direction, we're making positive progress.

Unfortunately, many of us compare our progress to that of others and worry that we aren't doing it right. We need to let each of our change journeys develop as uniquely as we ourselves do. So many factors contribute: the depth of our wounds, the support and helping resources available to us, and the level of our cooperation with the Spirit of God, to name a few. In fact, God is more realistic about all this than we are. (I suspect this is because He knows us perfectly while we labor under illusions of being stronger or weaker than we are.)

Speaking on behalf of God, the prophet Isaiah pictures three levels of functioning: (1) soaring on wings like eagles, (2) running and not growing weary, and (3) walking and not fainting (see Isaiah 40:31). I've noticed lately that I have fewer fainting days, a lot more running days, and even more soul-stretching soaring days than I used to have. But if I expected nothing but soaring, I'd be in big trouble.

Have your attempts at soaring crashed or sent you into a tailspin of disappointment? Remember, God understands and accepts you even if you are barely managing to walk without fainting. When I contemplate a lifelong process, I need a steadying, strengthening hope to sustain me for the long haul—especially when the process will hand me the agony of defeat at least as often as the thrill of victory.

We Need Hope

What fuels our lifelong mending, healing, changing journeys? The life-affirming nature planted within us by our living and life-giving God. God is committed to life from beginning to end.

God is the birther when we "must be born again" (John 3:7).

God is the healer when we've been wounded unto death.

God is the grave robber when we've buried our hopes for a bright future.

Our wise and loving God resurrects our hope because He knows, far more than we do, that without hope, we die. Even modern medical research confirms that hopelessness is deadly.[1] And many of us can personally testify that hopelessness *feels* deadly.

But what can we hope for? Certainly not for pain-free living. Even if our childhood wounders come to us and say, "Yes, I did it and I'm so sorry, please forgive me," and we do, we are still stuck with a life that has been shaped by the wounds. And in our misguided efforts at self-supervised healing, we add new wounds to the old—in ourselves and in those we love and don't want to hurt. No, we do not hope for life as if the wounds never happened. And we do not hope for the erasure of suffering.

God has a plan for the *effects* of our hurting and hurtful lives, the effects that we would prefer to have Him remove.

Stewardship of Weakness

God calls us to be good stewards—that is, wise managers. He means this for all aspects of our lives, including the weaknesses caused, in part, by our childhood wounds.

As I read my Bible, I find verse after verse where God asks us to bring to Him things like fears, cares, futures, and, yes, even our weaknesses. He wants us to bring Him our weakness so He can bear it for us. That's a far cry from what many of us think God wants to do with our weakness—especially if we were raised on the doctrine that real Christians are strong all the time.

Scripture tells us that God the Holy Spirit helps us "in our weakness" (Romans 8:26). He doesn't berate us for being weak; He helps us. The Greek term translated "help" portrays someone—the Spirit of God in this particular verse—coming alongside us to help us bear our burdens.

If that doesn't generate enough hope, there's more. God also promises to display His strength—the same strength that created the universe—in our times of weakness and pledges His "sufficient" grace at those times as well (2 Corinthians 12:9).

If we take seriously God's call to the stewardship of weakness, we learn this important truth: God does not abandon us when we need Him most. Instead, He comes alongside to help.

> **God does not abandon us when we need Him most. Instead, He comes alongside to help.**

Our fear of personal weakness evaporates like morning fog in the dazzling light of His strength and grace.

Weakness is one thing; suffering is another. And we may doubt that God can give us anything good when we give Him something bad—our suffering.

Stewardship of Suffering

Like aging, suffering does not necessarily improve people. It makes some folks better and others bitter. The difference isn't in the suffering; it's in the folks. More specifically, it's in what they do with the suffering.

God longs for us to come to Him with our sorrows and our suffering so that we'll know Him as Comforter.

We hear a lot more about our creator God than our comforter God. But He is both. And hurt people need to know more about the comforting part of God's nature. It's one thing to hear about divine comfort, but it's a quantum leap to experience it personally. I have good news and bad news about God's comfort.

> **We really will experience God's comfort when we suffer.**

The good news is this: *we really will experience God's comfort* when we suffer. Millions throughout the ages have testified to the reality of God's supernatural comfort. Count me among them.

The bad news is this: we really will experience God's comfort *when we suffer*. Said differently, God's comfort is the greatest show on earth, but the price of the ticket is sometimes fatal. What greater display of love could God give His children stranded for a spell on this sin-sick sphere than His comfort? And because we are not stranded alone, God tells us to be conduits of His comfort. We take in all we need and still have an overflow to share with others (2 Corinthians 1:3–4).

If God's comfort is so abundantly available, does that mean He erases all of our scars? I often get asked questions like this one at conferences or counseling sessions. Sometimes I'm asked, "Will I ever get over this?"

When we ask questions like this, we're actually looking for magic. We want to hear that we can live and function as though the hurt never happened.

But it did. And wounds leave scars. And even the scars factor into God's divine equation.

Stewardship of Scars

At the church our son and daughter-in-law used to attend, a woman signed to interpret the sermons for congregants who were deaf. I watched her graceful gestures one Sunday and wept when I realized the sign for Jesus. In rapid succession, she touched the palms of her open hands—first left, then right—with the middle finger of her opposite hand. The officially recognized sign for Jesus recalls the marks of His death.

Jesus is known by His scars. Ever since His wounding, death, and triumphant resurrection, Jesus has been identified by His scars. When timid Thomas couldn't believe the other disciples' resurrection news, Jesus invited him to believe the scars (John 20:24–29).

To all of us, Jesus identifies Himself by His scars. On a corpse, scars tell us how the person died. But Jesus comes to us alive; His scars speak of triumph over betrayal, victory over evil, life out of death, hope beyond despair.

As hurt people, we too wear scars. And God has a stewardship plan for our scars.

The subject of scars strikes close to home with me because I form what is called keloid tissue whenever I am cut—whether from carelessness or surgery. This means that instead of a nice thin line from an incision, I have something that looks more like a ridge of fleshy rope. Some scars whisper; mine shout.

The same is true of emotional and psychological scars. Some speak loudly, others softly, but they all have a history to tell. Good stewardship of our scars involves letting them tell *His* story. Letting our scars—the signs of our woundings—tell God's story is what Scripture calls offering up a "sacrifice of praise" (Hebrews 13:15).

> **Good stewardship of our scars involves letting them tell *His* story.**

I've heard a sacrifice described as giving up something we can't do without. Transferring that definition into the realm of language, a spoken sacrifice of praise is saying something we never could say. Never, that is, without God's supernatural intervention.

Never in my wildest nightmares could I have imagined traveling around the country telling total strangers about the most painful experiences of my life—showing them my scars, as it were. Every time I speak or write about them, I'm astounded to see how God is using for His glory the very things I grieved over and regretted most.

Those scars were a means not only to mold my character and to minister comfort to others but to tell the story of God's life-transforming grace and death-transcending power.

The Greatest Hope

"Is that it?" you ask. "Is that the best you have to offer in this 'hopeful tomorrows' chapter?"

I know that lofty promises of total healing and painless futures would sell more books. I have bought quite a few myself that had titles promising victory or triumph or total something or other.

Like me, many people go through life looking for contentment in a person, a cause, a career, a marriage, a child, a church, or some other contentment container. And, of course, we expect it to come with a lifetime guarantee.

Yet here we are, wounded and weary, our contentment containers dry. What a miserable, painful, exciting, hopeful place to be!

Only when we're at the end of ourselves will we reach for something beyond. Only when blinders of shame and bandages of perfectionism come off will we let God replace our unbearable yokes with His unbelievable grace. And only then can God's love pour in.

Of all hopes, this is the greatest: the promise of God's everlasting love. He plasters that promise from one end of His Word to the other. Jesus was the consummate container, the incandescent explainer of God's everlasting love. Just think of how Christ's ministry matches our misery. We come bruised, broken, and bound. Jesus comes healing, mending, and releasing. At this perfect fit of need and provision, we see the union of God's scars and God's everlasting love.

This very moment, God offers each of us His multifaceted, ever-living hope to comfort us, to encourage us, and to undergird each step of our journey from hurting to healing. He gives us so much:

- Hope that the stewardship of our weakness and suffering bring blessings to us and to others while bringing glory to God
- Hope that we will see more clearly how our wounding experiences fit His design for our lives
- Hope that as we embrace the reality of choice, change, and transformation, our scars will sing the praises of our living and loving Savior
- And, ultimately, hope that sees in the splintered fragments of our broken lives the reflection of His empty tomb

ACKNOWLEDGMENTS

Although I labored months to write every word of this book, many co-laborers have made it possible.

I deeply appreciate the good folks at Our Daily Bread Publishing who believed that the message of this book needed to be heard once again. I thank Dawn Anderson, Tim Gustafson, and especially Joel Armstrong for their valuable contributions.

As always, my dear husband earns a special word of gratitude. I wouldn't be doing any of this without his constant support and encouragement.

And to all of you who have shared your lives, your pain, and your healing adventures with me, please accept my sincere appreciation.

APPENDIX A: DISCOVERING YOUR TRUE IDENTITY

These verses will help you see yourself as God sees you. Read them prayerfully as you ask God to reveal your true identity.

- John 1:12; 1 Peter 2:9: I am God's child and I belong to Him.
- Romans 8:35–39: Nothing can separate me from God's love.
- Ephesians 1:4: I am chosen by God.
- Ephesians 2:18; 3:12: I have access to God through Jesus.
- Colossians 2:13–14: I am forgiven and my sin debt is paid.
- Romans 8:1: I am not condemned.
- Philippians 4:13: I am strengthened for all tasks to which God calls me.
- 1 Corinthians 6:19: My body is the Holy Spirit's abode.
- Romans 5:1: I have peace with God through Jesus Christ.

- Colossians 1:13: I have been rescued from the dominion of darkness and brought into the kingdom of God's Son.

Using your journal or a special notebook, write the verse, a personalized summary of the verse, and a past, present, or future application for it.

Your entries could follow this form:

> And you, being dead in your trespasses and the uncircumcision of your flesh, He has made alive together with Him, having forgiven you all trespasses, having wiped out the handwriting of requirements that was against us, which was contrary to us. And He has taken it out of the way, having nailed it to the cross. (Colossians 2:13–14 NKJV)

> *Because I am forgiven of all my sins, I don't need to continue to punish myself for sinful choices that I regret. God knows my heart, so He knows I have sincerely repented. That sin does not make me ineligible for God's gracious blessings.*

Begin memorizing the verses that are most meaningful to you. Perhaps you can get together with other Christian friends to study and discuss these verses and others that tell you how God sees you. In your local Christian bookstore or online, you can find Bible study guides available on this topic of seeing yourself as God sees you.

APPENDIX B: IDENTIFYING BELIEFS ABOUT EMOTIONS[1]

Shame-Bound Lie	Shame-Free Truth
Emotions are unnecessary, bothersome, unspiritual, and embarrassing. I need to work on eliminating them.	Emotions are a gift from God and an integral part of our human natures which reflect His image. Jesus came to take away our sins, not our feelings.
Emotions are bad and dangerous, so it is safer when I avoid them.	Emotions are neither good nor bad. They can be expressed appropriately, and I can learn to do that. I am less than the person God created me to be when I avoid feeling emotions.
If I begin to feel my emotions, I will lose it, fall apart, go crazy, or hurt someone.	When I am able to feel my emotions, I become more authentic and alive. Recognizing and expressing emotions may feel strange and scary at first, but I can find others who emote appropriately to help. I don't have to hurt anyone.

Shame-Bound Lie	Shame-Free Truth
It is stupid to get all upset over things that happened years ago. It is best to let sleeping dogs lie. Besides, none of that affects me now.	It is appropriate for children to feel confused, afraid, sad, and angry when their parents neglect or abuse them. Those feelings did not go away just because I had to learn to disown them. They are still inside, affecting my life today, and it is best to face them and feel them honestly.
When I felt sad as a child, no one was there for me. I couldn't stand to feel that despair and loneliness again. Besides, I am weak when I cry or act sad, and good Christians are never weak.	I have resources now as an adult that I did not have as a child. I can find more reliable (but imperfect) human comforters. And I know (or can know) God personally and have His comfort. Grieving childhood losses will be painful, but I can survive it.
When I was a child, I was told I should never be angry. I just know God is angry about my anger, both my anger about the past and my anger about present situations. Besides, good Christians never feel angry.	It is appropriate to feel angry about what angers God. Misleading or abusing children angers God. I can learn to express anger appropriately and without sinning (see Ephesians 4:26).

APPENDIX C: REPRESENTATIVE BIBLICAL PRINCIPLES OF RELATING

In your journal, list Bible verses expressing relationship principles along with their personal applications. Here are a few examples.

When Jesus saw him lying there and learned that he had been in this condition for a long time, he asked him, "Do you want to get well?" (John 5:6)	*Principle:* Jesus didn't invade a needy man's personal boundaries. *Personal Application Example:* When I'm helping people, I need to respect them and their personal boundaries enough to ask them what they want me to do for them.
Then, because so many people were coming and going that they did not even have a chance to eat, he [Jesus] said to them, "Come with me by yourselves to a quiet place and get some rest." (Mark 6:31)	*Principle:* Jesus encourages people helpers to take care of themselves. *Personal Application Example:* It's all right for me to say no sometimes when I'm too exhausted to accept a task someone asks me to take—even at church.

Jesus said, "Let the little children come to me, and do not hinder them." (Matthew 19:14)	*Principle:* Jesus didn't let people tell Him what to do (e.g., send children away). *Personal Application Example:* It's okay when I hold my own opinions, even when others disagree. I don't have to hide my views or values to be congenial or kind.
If it is possible, as far as it depends on you, live at peace with everyone. (Romans 12:18)	*Principle:* We should aim for peaceful relationships. But the phrase "as far as it depends on you" recognizes the truth that we can't control others' choices. *Personal Application Example:* I want peace with my boyfriend, but I can't control his choices, even when I violate my standards to do everything he asks.
Let us therefore make every effort to do what leads to peace and to mutual edification. (Romans 14:19)	*Principle:* Peace is not God's only relationship goal. He wants our relationships to be balanced and to produce mutual growth. *Personal Application Example:* I am the principal caretaker and giver in 90 percent of my relationships. I am going to look for people who are willing to have more balance and mutuality in our friendships.
Carry each other's burdens, and in this way you will fulfill the law of Christ. . . . For each one should carry their own load. (Galatians 6:2, 5)	*Principle:* We should handle our normal loads with a degree of independence from others but also be willing to give and receive help in overburdening situations. This is healthy, balanced interdependence. *Personal Application Example:* I never let friends help me in my overburdened times. I always want to be the wise and strong one. I feel embarrassed and weak when I think about asking someone to help me, yet I am always trying to convince others that it's okay for them to accept my help.

APPENDIX D: SOME ATTRIBUTES OF GOD[1]

- *God is compassionate*, as demonstrated in His mercy and loving-kindness. "The LORD is compassionate and gracious, slow to anger, abounding in love" (Psalm 103:8).
- *God is forgiving* because of His grace and mercy. Jesus paid our sin debts so that God could forgive sin while remaining holy and just. "In him [Christ] we have redemption through his blood, the forgiveness of sins, in accordance with the riches of God's grace" (Ephesians 1:7; see also Romans 3:23–26).
- *God is immutable*; He never changes. "Jesus Christ is the same yesterday and today and forever" (Hebrews 13:8).
- *God is loving* because of His nature and not because of anything we do to elicit His love. His love is expressed in actions toward us. "God is love" (1 John 4:16).
- *God is omnipotent* because He has unlimited power and ability. "You have made the heavens and the earth by

your great power and outstretched arm. Nothing is too hard for you" (Jeremiah 32:17).

- *God is omnipresent* because He is present everywhere in the universe at the same time. God is never absent. "'Am I only a God nearby,' declares the LORD, 'and not a God far away? Who can hide in secret places so that I cannot see them?' declares the LORD. 'Do not I fill heaven and earth?' declares the LORD" (Jeremiah 23:23–24).

- *God is omniscient* because of His unlimited knowledge and wisdom. "You know when I sit and when I rise; you perceive my thoughts from afar. You discern my going out and my lying down; you are familiar with all my ways. Before a word is on my tongue you, LORD, know it completely" (Psalm 139:2–4).

- *God is righteous* because He only does what is right and is free from any wrongdoing. "The LORD is righteous in all his ways and faithful in all he does" (Psalm 145:17).

- *God is sovereign* because He rules supremely over all creation. "He does as he pleases with the powers of heaven and the peoples of the earth. No one can hold back his hand or say to him: 'What have you done?'" (Daniel 4:35).

APPENDIX E: SHAME-BASED VERSUS GRACE-BASED CHURCHES[1]

Shame-Full Church Family *Some-Grace Theology*	Grace-Full Church Family *All-Grace Theology*
God is presented as a demanding Pharisee-Shepherd who drives His sheep.	God is presented as an understanding Father-Shepherd who leads His sheep.
Once, by God's grace, we trust in Jesus's righteousness to pay for our sins, God's acceptance is earned by performing and pleasing with our own good works and law keeping.	From beginning to end, God's acceptance is solely the gift of His grace, which we receive by trusting in Jesus's perfect work of fulfilling the law and dying to pay the penalty for our sins.
I am expected to be totally (or almost totally) transformed the moment I trust Christ.	I am expected to keep on being transformed by having my mind renewed as long as I live.
Since I should be totally transformed (i.e., perfect), I am a different and worthless Christian because I'm not perfect.	Since I am in a lifelong process of being transformed to be like Jesus, my imperfections don't surprise either me or God.

Shame-Full Church Family *Some-Grace Theology*	Grace-Full Church Family *All-Grace Theology*
Members with obvious problems are an embarrassment to our church. Since real Christians have no serious problems, we don't need to bother making any provisions to help.	Members with obvious problems are expected since the past and present effects of sin in Christians' lives can cause serious problems. There are programs in place to provide appropriate help.
Small group Bible studies are dangerous places because someone might get close enough to see behind my mask of perfection and know I have problems.	Small group Bible studies are safe places to practice being maskless and real with others who do the same. It's great to go where I don't have to hide my problems.
The emphasis is on looking religious by wearing the right clothes and carrying the right translation of the Bible.	The emphasis is on developing a deeper relationship of love and trusting obedience with the Lord Jesus Christ.
The emphasis is on revealing and rebuking sinners.	The emphasis is on restoring repentant sinners.
Attendance at church activities is used as the main indicator of a person's true spirituality.	True spirituality is reflected in one's total lifestyle and known only to God.

NOTES

Introduction

1. Ateret Gewirtz-Meydan and David Finkelhor, "Sexual Abuse and Assault in a Large National Sample of Children and Adolescents," *Child Maltreatment* 25, no. 2 (2020): 203–14.
2. "Michigan: Fatal Overreaction," *Time*, August 19, 1989, https://content.time.com/time/subscriber/article/0,33009,958326,00.html.

Chapter 1: Unseen Wounds

1. To learn more about shame, its origins, effects, and solutions, see my book *Released from Shame: Moving beyond the Pain of the Past*, rev. ed. (Downers Grove, IL: InterVarsity Press, 2002).

Chapter 2: The Problem of Unseen Wounds

1. See, for instance, Jason M. Armfield et al., "Intergenerational Transmission of Child Maltreatment in South Australia, 1986–2017: A Retrospective Cohort Study," *Lancet Public Health* 6, no. 7 (July 2021): E450–61, https://doi.org/10.1016/S2468-2667(21)00024-4; Alan R. King et al., "Revisiting the Link between Childhood Sexual Abuse and Adult Sexual Aggression, *Child Abuse and Neglect* 94 (June

2019): https://doi.org/10.1016/j.chiabu.2019.104022; and
Ashley F. Jespersen, Martin L. Lalumière, and Michael C.
Seto, "Sexual Abuse History among Adult Sex Offenders
and Non-Sex Offenders: A Meta-Analysis," *Child Abuse and
Neglect* 33, no. 3 (March 2009): 179–92, https://doi.org
/10.1016/j.chiabu.2008.07.004.

Chapter 3: Hurt by the Unprepared and Unavailable

1. This description of biological shame is adapted from my
   book *Released from Shame: Moving beyond the Pain of the
   Past*, rev. ed. (Downers Grove, IL: InterVarsity Press, 2002),
   24–25.
2. Lane Strathearn et al., "Long-Term Cognitive, Psychological, and Health Outcomes Associated with Child Abuse
   and Neglect," *Pediatrics* 146, no. 4 (October 2020): 389–403,
   https://doi.org/10.1542/peds.2020-0438.

Chapter 4: Hurt by Liars and Thieves

1. John Friel and Linda Friel, *Adult Children: The Secrets of Dysfunctional Families* (Deerfield Beach, FL: Health Communi-
   cations, 1988), 35–36.
2. David Finkelhor et al., "The Lifetime Prevalence of Child
   Sexual Abuse and Sexual Assault Assessed in Late Adolescence," *Journal of Adolescent Health* 55, no. 3 (2014): 329–33.
3. "Children and Teens: Statistics," RAINN, accessed August 6,
   2024, https://www.rainn.org/statistics/children-and-teens.
4. Associated Press, "Clown Draws 10-Year Sentence," *Cincinnati Enquirer*, December 15, 1991, D-2.

Chapter 6: Hurt by Childhood Choices

1. Walter Bauer, William Arndt, and F. Wilbur Gingrich, *A
   Greek-English Lexicon of the New Testament*, 2nd ed. (University of Chicago Press, 1979), 752.

Chapter 7: Help for Healing Our Hurts

1. Earnie Larsen, *What I Practice, I Become* (St. Paul, MN: International Marriage Encounter, 1986), 17.
2. David Seamands, *Putting Away Childish Things* (Wheaton, IL: Victor Books, 1982), 5.
3. Walter Bauer, William Arndt, and F. Wilbur Gingrich, *A Greek-English Lexicon of the New Testament*, 2nd ed. (University of Chicago Press, 1979), 417.
4. "Quotes from Philip," PKotler.org, accessed August 6, 2024, https://www.pkotler.org/quotes-from-pk.

Chapter 8: Help for Healing Self-Inflicted Wounds

1. Lucy Cousins, "Can Always Staying Positive Be Bad for Our Health?," Hospitals Contribution Fund of Australia, August 2022, https://www.hcf.com.au/health-agenda/body-mind/mental-health/downsides-to-always-being-positive.
2. Jeff VanVonderen, *Tired of Trying to Measure Up: Getting Free from the Demands, Expectations, and Intimidation of Well-Meaning People* (Minneapolis, MN: Bethany, 1989), 20.

Chapter 9: Help for Healing Friends and Spouses

1. Associated Press, "Assault in Adolescence Leads to Higher Risk of Rape," *Cincinnati Enquirer*, August 17, 1992, A-3.
2. Scripture declares that all human hearts are "deceitful above all things" (Jeremiah 17:9), and this means that any person's deceitful heart has the potential for enormous evil.
3. This chart is adapted from one that appeared previously in my book *Released from Shame: Moving beyond the Pain of the Past*, rev. ed. (Downers Grove, IL: InterVarsity Press, 2002), 130.
4. This chart appeared previously in Wilson, *Released from Shame*, 133.
5. "Marriage and Cohabitation in the US," Pew Research Center, November 6, 2019, https://www.pewresearch.org/social-trends/2019/11/06/marriage-and-cohabitation-in-the-u-s/.

6. Scott M. Stanley and Galena K. Rhoades, "What's the Plan? Cohabitation, Engagement, and Divorce," Institute for Family Studies, April 2023, https://ifstudies.org/ifs-admin/resources/reports/cohabitationreportapr2023-final.pdf.

7. Herbert Gravits and Julie Bowden, *Guide to Recovery: A Book for Adult Children of Alcoholics* (Holmes Beach, FL: Learning Publications, 1985), 73.

Chapter 10: Help for Healing Leaders

1. Tom Barrett, unpublished doctoral dissertation for Union Institute and University. Most of the insights about employment-home conflict are taken from this document.

2. "Statistics," Not in Our Church, accessed August 6, 2024, https://www.notinourchurch.com/statistics.html; "Alarming Numbers," Stop Baptist Predators, accessed August 6, 2024, https://stopbaptistpredators.org/alarmingnumbers.html.

3. David Johnson and Jeff VanVonderen, *The Subtle Power of Spiritual Abuse* (Minneapolis, MN: Bethany, 1991), 103.

4. J. I. Packer, *Rediscovering Holiness: Know the Fullness of Life with God*, 2nd ed. (Ventura, CA: Regal, 2009), 41.

5. I heard Dr. Archibald Hart say this at a consultation on "Pastors in Crisis."

Chapter 11: Help for Healing Followers

1. J. I. Packer, *Rediscovering Holiness: Know the Fullness of Life with God*, 2nd ed. (Ventura, CA: Regal, 2009), 41.

2. Susan Hogan-Albach, "Pastors Struggle to Draw Relationship Boundaries," *Cincinnati Enquirer*, September 9, 1992, D-5.

3. Yongshun Cai, "Community Elites and Collective Action: The State and the Starved during the Chinese Famine (1959–61)," *Politics and Society* 48, no. 1 (2020): 108.

4. Jeff VanVonderen, *Tired of Trying to Measure Up: Getting Free from the Demands, Expectations, and Intimidation of Well-Meaning People* (Minneapolis, MN: Bethany, 1989), 87.

Chapter 12: Help for Hurting Worshipers

1. *Cincinnati Enquirer*, August 25, 1992, East Central Extra, 2.
2. This exercise first appeared in my book *Shame-Free Parenting* (Westmont, IL: InterVarsity Press, 1992). I am indebted to Dr. Ray DuPont for suggesting it.
3. Ann Trebbe, "Charting a 90s Path to Self-Help," *USA Today*, June 20, 1991, 1-D. Emphasis added.

Chapter 13: Help for Healing Forgivers

1. Colin Brown, ed., *The New International Dictionary of New Testament Theology*, vol. 1 (Grand Rapids, MI: Zondervan, 1986), 697.
2. Arnold Fox and Barry Fox, "The Gift of Forgiveness: Giving Up the Emotional Toxins," *Changes*, May–June 1989, 18.

Chapter 14: Help for Healing Parents

1. This chart is from my book *Shame-Free Parenting* (Westmont, IL: InterVarsity Press, 1992), 41.
2. Wilson, *Shame-Free Parenting*, 104–5.
3. Wilson, *Shame-Free Parenting*, 118.

Chapter 15: Help for Hopeful Tomorrows

1. Igor Marchetti, Lauren B. Alloy, and Ernst H. W. Koster, "Breaking the Vise of Hopelessness: Targeting Its Components, Antecedents, and Context," *International Journal of Cognitive Therapy* 16 (2023): 285–319. See also Rita Gruber and Manuel Schwanda, "Hopelessness during Acute Hospitalisation Is a Strong Predictor of Mortality," *Evidence-Based Nursing* 24, no. 2 (2021): 53.

Appendix B: Identifying Beliefs about Emotions

1. This chart is adapted from one that appears in my book *Released from Shame: Moving beyond the Pain of the Past*, rev. ed. (Downers Grove, IL: InterVarsity Press, 2002), 115.

Appendix D: Some Attributes of God

1. This list is from my book *Released from Shame: Moving beyond the Pain of the* Past, rev. ed. (Downers Grove, IL: InterVarsity Press, 2002), 193–94.

Appendix E: Shame-Based versus Grace-Based Churches

1. This chart is adapted from one that appears in my book *Released from Shame: Moving beyond the Pain of the Past*, rev. ed. (Downers Grove, IL: InterVarsity Press, 2002), 151.

Seek and she will find.

You'll be reminded that you are intimately known and deeply loved by your heavenly Father when you spend time with Him while reading *God Hears Her*. The personal stories, along with Scripture passages and inspirational quotes, reassure you that you are heard, cherished, and enough—no matter what you're going through.

How do you deepen your relationship with and understanding of God?

At the source.
Get to know Him through His own Word, the Bible.

Know Him devotes 365 days to revealing the character of God solely through Scripture. These passages, drawn from every book of the Bible, highlight 12 unchanging attributes of our Creator. Whether you're new to the Bible or a longtime reader, you'll gain a deeper awe of God's holiness, transcendence, and glory along with a renewed appreciation for His mercy, justice, and truth.

Buy It Today

BE STRONG

IN THE POWER OF GOD

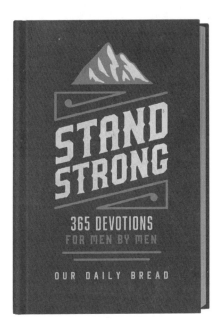

This collection of personal stories and relevant Scriptures will inspire you to grow in your relationship with God, live a life of integrity, and embrace God's strength in every area of your life.

Spread the Word
by Doing One Thing.

- Give a copy of this book as a gift.

- Share the QR code link via your social media.

- Write a review of this book on your blog, favorite bookseller's website, or at ourdailybreadpublishing.org.

- Recommend this book to your church, small group, or book club.

Connect with us. 🄵 🄾

Our Daily Bread Publishing
PO Box 3566, Grand Rapids, MI 49501, USA
Email: books@odbm.org

Love God. Love Others.

with  Our Daily Bread.

Your gift changes lives.

Connect with us. f ⊡

Our Daily Bread Publishing
PO Box 3566, Grand Rapids, MI 49501, USA
Email: books@odbm.org